TO

....

FROM

....

DATE

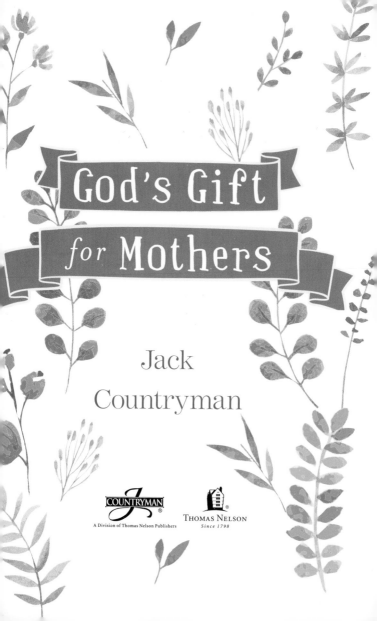

God's Gift for Mothers

Jack Countryman

COUNTRYMAN ®

A Division of Thomas Nelson Publishers

THOMAS NELSON

Since 1798

Published in Nashville, Tennessee, by Thomas Nelson®. Thomas Nelson is a registered trademark of HarperCollins Christian Publishing, Inc.

Scripture quotations are taken from the New King James Version®. © 1982 by Thomas Nelson. Used by permission. All rights reserved.

Cover design by Studio Gearbox
Interior design by Kristy Edwards

ISBN-13: 978-0-7180-8999-3

Printed in China

17 18 19 20 21 TIMS 5 4 3 2 1

Introduction

A mother is the centerpiece of any family. She takes care of the children by providing for their well-being and giving them the love that they need. She cares for the rest of the family's needs as well. My life has been blessed with the gifts of a godly mother and a godly wife. Both have influenced my life and helped me become a man who walks with God. This book has been designed to open the eyes and guide the reader to be a godly mother. *God's Gift for Mothers* is a Scripture-led book that demonstrates the love God has for all mothers. May you be filled with His presence as you read through these pages.

Contents

The Responsibility of Motherhood

The Promises of Motherhood

The Blessings of Motherhood

Scripture Meditations for Mothers

God's Answers for Mothers

God Comforts Mothers as They Learn to . . .

God Freely Gives to Mothers . . .

God Rejoices with Mothers When They . . .

God Walks with Mothers . . .

God Delights in Mothers Who Are . . .

Prominent Mothers in the Bible

Bathsheba

MOTHER OF SOLOMON

Then David comforted Bathsheba his wife, and went in to her and lay with her. So she bore a son, and he called his name Solomon.

—2 SAMUEL 12:24

Go forth, O daughters of Zion,
And see King Solomon with the crown
With which his mother crowned him
On the day of his wedding,
The day of the gladness of his heart.

—SONG OF SOLOMON 3:11

*Then she said to him, "My lord, you swore by
the Lord your God to your maidservant, saying,
'Assuredly Solomon your son shall reign after me,
and he shall sit on my throne.'" . . . Then King David
answered and said, "Call Bathsheba to me." So she
came into the king's presence and stood before the
king. And the king took an oath and said, "As the
Lord lives, who has redeemed my life from every
distress, just as I swore to you by the Lord God of
Israel, saying, 'Assuredly Solomon your son shall be
king after me, and he shall sit on my throne in my
place,' so I certainly will do this day." Then Bathsheba
bowed with her face to the earth, and paid homage
to the king, and said, "Let my lord King David live
forever!"*

—1 Kings 1:17, 28–31

Elizabeth

MOTHER OF JOHN THE BAPTIST

There was in the days of Herod, the king of Judea, a certain priest named Zacharias, of the division of Abijah. His wife was of the daughters of Aaron, and her name was Elizabeth. And they were both righteous before God, walking in all the commandments and ordinances of the Lord blameless. But they had no child, because Elizabeth was barren, and they were both well advanced in years. . . . But the angel said to him, "Do not be afraid, Zacharias, for your prayer is heard; and your wife Elizabeth will bear you a son, and you shall call his name John."

—LUKE 1:5–7, 13

Now indeed, Elizabeth your relative has also conceived a son in her old age; and this is now the sixth month for her who was called barren. For with God nothing will be impossible.

—LUKE 1:36–37

Eve

MOTHER OF ALL LIVING

*And Adam called his wife's name Eve, because
she was the mother of all living.*

*—*Genesis 3:20

*Now Adam knew Eve his wife, and she con-
ceived and bore Cain, and said, "I have
acquired a man from the* Lord.*" Then she bore
again, this time his brother Abel. Now Abel was
a keeper of sheep, but Cain was a tiller of the
ground.*

*—*Genesis 4:1–2

*And Adam knew his wife again, and she bore
a son and named him Seth, "For God has
appointed another seed for me instead of Abel,
whom Cain killed."*

*—*Genesis 4:25

Hannah

MOTHER OF SAMUEL

*And she was in bitterness of soul, and prayed to the L*ORD *and wept in anguish. Then she made a vow and said, "O L*ORD *of hosts, if You will indeed look on the affliction of Your maidservant and remember me . . . but will give Your maidservant a male child, then I will give him to the L*ORD *all the days of his life, and no razor shall come upon his head."*

—1 SAMUEL 1:10–11

*For this child I prayed, and the L*ORD *has granted me my petition which I asked of Him. Therefore I also have lent him to the L*ORD*; as long as he lives he shall be lent to the L*ORD.

—1 SAMUEL 1:27–28

*And the L*ORD *visited Hannah, so that she conceived and bore three sons and two daughters. Meanwhile the child Samuel grew before the L*ORD.

—1 SAMUEL 2:21

Jochebed

MOTHER OF MOSES, AARON,
AND MIRIAM

*And a man of the house of Levi went and took
as wife a daughter of Levi. So the woman
conceived and bore a son. And when she saw
that he was a beautiful child, she hid him three
months. But when she could no longer hide him,
she took an ark of bulrushes for him, daubed it
with asphalt and pitch, put the child in it, and
laid it in the reeds by the river's bank. And his
sister stood afar off, to know what would be
done to him.*

—EXODUS 2:1–4

*The name of Amram's wife was Jochebed the
daughter of Levi, who was born to Levi in
Egypt; and to Amram she bore Aaron and
Moses and their sister Miriam.*

—NUMBERS 26:59

Leah

MOTHER OF REUBEN, SIMEON,
LEVI, JUDAH, ZEBULON, DINAH,
AND ISSACHAR

When the LORD saw that Leah was unloved, He opened her womb; but Rachel was barren. So Leah conceived and bore a son, and she called his name Reuben; for she said, "The LORD has surely looked on my affliction. Now therefore, my husband will love me." Then she conceived again and bore a son, and said, "Because the LORD has heard that I am unloved, He has therefore given me this son also." And she called his name Simeon. She conceived again and bore a son, and said, "Now this time my husband will become attached to me, because I have borne him three sons." Therefore his name was called Levi. And she conceived again and bore a son, and said, "Now I will praise the LORD." Therefore she called his name Judah. Then she stopped bearing.

—GENESIS 29:31–35

And God listened to Leah, and she conceived and bore Jacob a fifth son. Leah said, "God has given me my wages, because I have given my maid to my husband." So she called his name Issachar. Then Leah conceived again and bore Jacob a sixth son. And Leah said, "God has endowed me with a good endowment; now my husband will dwell with me, because I have borne him six sons." So she called his name Zebulun. Afterward she bore a daughter, and called her name Dinah.

—GENESIS 30:17–21

Mary

MOTHER OF JESUS

*Now the birth of Jesus Christ was as follows:
After His mother Mary was betrothed to Joseph,
before they came together, she was found
with child of the Holy Spirit. Then Joseph her
husband, being a just man, and not wanting to
make her a public example, was minded to put
her away secretly. But while he thought about
these things, behold, an angel of the Lord appeared to him in a dream, saying, "Joseph, son
of David, do not be afraid to take to you Mary
your wife, for that which is conceived in her is of
the Holy Spirit. And she will bring forth a Son,
and you shall call His name JESUS, for He will
save His people from their sins."*

—MATTHEW 1:18–21

*Now in the sixth month the angel Gabriel was sent
by God to a city of Galilee named Nazareth, to a
virgin betrothed to a man whose name was Joseph,
of the house of David. The virgin's name was Mary.
And having come in, the angel said to her, "Rejoice,
highly favored one, the Lord is with you; blessed are
you among women!" But when she saw him, she was
troubled at his saying, and considered what manner of
greeting this was. Then the angel said to her, "Do not
be afraid, Mary, for you have found favor with God.
And behold, you will conceive in your womb and bring
forth a Son, and shall call His name Jesus."*

—Luke 1:26–31

*Now there stood by the cross of Jesus His mother, and
His mother's sister, Mary the wife of Clopas, and Mary
Magdalene. When Jesus therefore saw His mother, and
the disciple whom He loved standing by, He said to
His mother, "Woman, behold your son!" Then He said
to the disciple, "Behold your mother!" And from that
hour that disciple took her to his own home.*

—John 19:25–27

Naomi

MOTHER-IN-LAW OF RUTH

And Naomi said to her two daughters-in-law, "Go, return each to her mother's house. The LORD deal kindly with you, as you have dealt with the dead and with me. The LORD grant that you may find rest, each in the house of her husband." So she kissed them, and they lifted up their voices and wept.

—RUTH 1:8–9

Orpah kissed her mother-in-law, but Ruth clung to her. . . . Ruth said:

"Entreat me not to leave you,
    Or to turn back from following after you;
    For wherever you go, I will go;
    And wherever you lodge, I will lodge;
    Your people shall be my people,
    And your God, my God.
    Where you die, I will die,
    And there will I be buried."

—RUTH 1:14, 16–17

Rachel

MOTHER OF JOSEPH AND BENJAMIN

Now when Rachel saw that she bore Jacob no
children, Rachel envied her sister, and said to
Jacob, "Give me children, or else I die!"

—Genesis 30:1

Then God remembered Rachel, and God
listened to her and opened her womb. And she
conceived and bore a son, and said, "God has
taken away my reproach." So she called his
name Joseph, and said, "The Lord shall add to
me another son."

—Genesis 30:22–24

Ruth

MOTHER OF OBED

*Moreover, Ruth the Moabitess, the widow
of Mahlon, I have acquired as my wife, to
perpetuate the name of the dead through his
inheritance, that the name of the dead may not
be cut off from among his brethren and from his
position at the gate. You are witnesses this day.*

—Ruth 4:10

*So Boaz took Ruth and she became his wife;
and when he went in to her, the Lord gave her
conception, and she bore a son. Then the women
said to Naomi, "Blessed be the Lord, who has
not left you this day without a close relative; and
may his name be famous in Israel! And may he
be to you a restorer of life and a nourisher of your
old age; for your daughter-in-law, who loves you,
who is better to you than seven sons, has borne
him." Then Naomi took the child and laid him
on her bosom, and became a nurse to him.*

—Ruth 4:13–16

Sarah

MOTHER OF ISAAC

Then God said to Abraham, "As for Sarai your wife, you shall not call her name Sarai, but Sarah shall be her name. And I will bless her and also give you a son by her; then I will bless her, and she shall be a mother of nations; kings of peoples shall be from her."

—GENESIS 17:15–16

Then God said: "No, Sarah your wife shall bear you a son, and you shall call his name Isaac; I will establish My covenant with him for an everlasting covenant, and with his descendants after him."

—GENESIS 17:19

Abigail

WIFE OF DAVID

And David sent and proposed to Abigail, to take her as his wife. When the servants of David had come to Abigail at Carmel, they spoke to her saying, "David sent us to you, to ask you to become his wife." Then she arose, bowed her face to the earth, and said, "Here is your maidservant, a servant to wash the feet of the servants of my lord." So Abigail rose in haste and rode on a donkey, attended by five of her maidens; and she followed the messengers of David, and became his wife.

—1 Samuel 25:39–42

Mothers'
Prayers from
the Bible

Deborah

PRAYER OF PRAISE

*Then Deborah and Barak the son of Abinoam
sang on that day, saying:*

"When leaders lead in Israel,
When the people willingly offer themselves,
Bless the Lord!
Hear, O kings! Give ear, O princes!
I, even I, will sing to the Lord;
I will sing praise to the Lord God of Israel.
Lord, when You went out from Seir,
When You marched from the field of Edom,
The earth trembled and the heavens
poured,
The clouds also poured water;
The mountains gushed before the Lord,
This Sinai, before the Lord God of
Israel. . . .
I, Deborah, arose,
Arose a mother in Israel."

—Judges 5:1–5, 7

Hagar

PRAYER FOR THE LIFE OF HER CHILD

*Then she went and sat down across from him
at a distance of about a bowshot; for she said to
herself, "Let me not see the death of the boy." So
she sat opposite him, and lifted her voice and
wept. And God heard the voice of the lad. Then
the angel of God called to Hagar out of heaven,
and said to her, "What ails you, Hagar? Fear
not, for God has heard the voice of the lad where
he is. Arise, lift up the lad and hold him with
your hand, for I will make him a great nation."
Then God opened her eyes, and she saw a well
of water. And she went and filled the skin with
water, and gave the lad a drink.*

—GENESIS 21:16–19

Hannah

PRAYER TO HEAL HER BARRENNESS
AND TO GIVE HER A SON

*So Hannah arose after they had finished eating
and drinking in Shiloh. Now Eli the priest was
sitting on the seat by the doorpost of the tabernacle of the LORD. And she was in bitterness of
soul, and prayed to the LORD and wept in anguish. Then she made a vow and said, "O LORD
of hosts, if You will indeed look on the affliction
of Your maidservant and remember me, and
not forget Your maidservant, but will give Your
maidservant a male child, then I will give him
to the LORD all the days of his life, and no razor
shall come upon his head."*

—1 SAMUEL 1:9–11

*Then they slaughtered a bull, and brought the
child to Eli. And she said, "O my lord! As your
soul lives, my lord, I am the woman who stood
by you here, praying to the LORD. For this child*

I prayed, and the LORD has granted me my petition which I asked of Him. Therefore I also have lent him to the LORD; as long as he lives he shall be lent to the LORD." So they worshiped the LORD there.

—1 SAMUEL 1:25–28

And Hannah prayed and said:

"My heart rejoices in the LORD;
    My horn is exalted in the LORD.
    I smile at my enemies,
    Because I rejoice in Your salvation.
    No one is holy like the LORD,
    For there is none besides You,
    Nor is there any rock like our God.
    Talk no more so very proudly;
    Let no arrogance come from your mouth,
    For the LORD is the God of knowledge;
    And by Him actions are weighed."

—1 SAMUEL 2:1–3

Mary

PRAYER OF PRAISE

And Mary said:

"My soul magnifies the Lord,
*   And my spirit has rejoiced in God my*
*   Savior.*
*   For He has regarded the lowly state of His*
*   maidservant;*
*   For behold, henceforth all generations will*
*   call me blessed.*
*   For He who is mighty has done great things*
*   for me,*
*   And holy is His name.*
*   And His mercy is on those who fear Him*
*   From generation to generation.*
*   He has shown strength with His arm;*
*   He has scattered the proud in the imagina-*
*   tion of their hearts.*
*   He has put down the mighty from their*
*   thrones,*

And exalted the lowly.
He has filled the hungry with good things,
And the rich He has sent away empty.
He has helped His servant Israel,
In remembrance of His mercy,
As He spoke to our fathers,
To Abraham and to his seed forever."

—LUKE 1:46–55

Canaanite Mother

PRAYER FOR A DEMON-POSSESSED CHILD

And behold, a woman of Canaan came from that region and cried out to Him, saying, "Have mercy on me, O Lord, Son of David! My daughter is severely demon-possessed." But He answered her not a word. And His disciples came and urged Him, saying, "Send her away, for she cries out after us." But He answered and said, "I was not sent except to the lost sheep of the house of Israel." Then she came and worshiped Him, saying, "Lord, help me!" But He answered and said, "It is not good to take the children's bread and throw it to the little dogs." And she said, "Yes, Lord, yet even the little dogs eat the crumbs which fall from their masters' table." Then Jesus answered and said to her, "O woman, great is your faith! Let it be to you as you desire." And her daughter was healed from that very hour.

—Matthew 15:22–28

Elijah on Behalf of the Zarephath Widow

PRAYER FOR LIFE

Now it happened after these things that the son of the woman who owned the house became sick. And his sickness was so serious that there was no breath left in him. So she said to Elijah, "What have I to do with you, O man of God? Have you come to me to bring my sin to remembrance, and to kill my son?" And he said to her, "Give me your son." So he took him out of her arms and carried him to the upper room where he was staying, and laid him on his own bed. Then he cried out to the Lord *and said, "O* Lord *my God, have You also brought tragedy on the widow with whom I lodge, by killing her son?" And he stretched himself out on the child three times, and cried out to the* Lord *and said, "O* Lord *my God, I pray, let this child's soul come back to him." Then the* Lord *heard the voice of Elijah; and the soul of the child came back to him, and he revived.*

—1 Kings 17:17–22

The
Responsibility
of Motherhood

Commitment

Motherhood is a great and awesome—sometimes overwhelming—responsibility. When we talk about the responsibility of motherhood, the word *commitment* plays an important role in the life of a mother. Commitment means being dedicated to a task. When you are all in and totally committed to your children, your whole demeanor will change, and your children will become a major part of your life. When they are very young, the commitment is a twenty-four-hour task. As they grow, the requirements of motherhood change, but you remain committed to caring for your children and acting in their best interests, even when they rebel. Commitment is essential to the success of every mother, for out of commitment comes the fruit of fulfillment and happiness.

"Can a woman forget her nursing child,
    And not have compassion on the son of her womb?
    Surely they may forget,
    Yet I will not forget you.
    See, I have inscribed you on the palms of My hands;
    Your walls are continually before Me."

          —Isaiah 49:15–16

Who can find a virtuous wife?
    For her worth is far above rubies.
    The heart of her husband safely trusts her;
    So he will have no lack of gain.
    She does him good and not evil
    All the days of her life.
    She seeks wool and flax,
    And willingly works with her hands.
    She is like the merchant ships,
    She brings her food from afar.
    She also rises while it is yet night,
    And provides food for her household.

          —Proverbs 31:10–15

Compassion

Compassion is an awareness of another's suffering and a desire to help. When compassion is a part of your life, your love for your children flows naturally from you. The Lord has chosen to be compassionate to those who choose to follow Him. Just as God is compassionate toward you, you will want to show compassion to your children so that they will see and feel the love that you have for them every day. By following your example, they will learn how to be compassionate. When you tell your children that you love them, it will make them feel secure, and their self-image will grow in a positive and healthy way.

And when she opened it, she saw the child, and behold, the baby wept. So she had compassion on him, and said, "This is one of the Hebrews' children." Then his sister said to Pharaoh's daughter, "Shall I go and call a nurse for you from the Hebrew women, that she may nurse the child for you?" And Pharaoh's daughter said to her, "Go." So the maiden went and called the child's mother. Then Pharaoh's daughter said to her, "Take this child away and nurse him for me, and I will give you your wages." So the woman took the child and nursed him. And the child grew, and she brought him to Pharaoh's daughter, and he became her son. So she called his name Moses, saying, "Because I drew him out of the water."

—Exodus 2:6–10

She stretches out her hands to the distaff,
    And her hand holds the spindle.
    She extends her hand to the poor,
    Yes, she reaches out her hands to the needy.
—Proverbs 31:19–20

Discipline

The word *discipline* comes from the Latin words for *teach* and *learn*. Christ's disciples were those whom He taught, meaning they learned discipline from Him as well as His teachings. When you discipline your children, you are teaching them the way to go. Correcting your children is a part of the responsibility of a mother. When you correct the behavior of your children, you are doing them a favor. As they grow, they need to understand the difference between right and wrong behavior. If correction is difficult for you, remember that what you are doing is for the benefit of your children. They need to know what acceptable behavior is and what it is not. If you take a stand when your children are young, then you will have disciplined children, and this is in your children's best interests.

*For whom the L*ORD *loves He corrects.*

> *Just as a father the son in whom he delights.*

> > —PROVERBS 3:12

The rod and rebuke give wisdom,

> *But a child left to himself brings shame to his mother.*
> *When the wicked are multiplied, transgression increases;*
> *But the righteous will see their fall.*
> *Correct your son, and he will give you rest;*
> *Yes, he will give delight to your soul.*

> > —PROVERBS 29:15–17

She girds herself with strength,

> *And strengthens her arms.*
> *She perceives that her merchandise is good,*
> *And her lamp does not go out by night. . . .*
> *She watches over the ways of her household,*
> *And does not eat the bread of idleness.*

> > —PROVERBS 31:17–18, 27

Example

You are the mirror that your children look into every day as they grow. The way you talk, walk, and act will be a reflection of who your children will become. Therefore, the love that you show must be open, sincere, and caring. Telling your children how much they mean to you often builds bridges that will stand the test of time. Your children will grow up respecting their parents. Then they can be examples to others. You are also a mirror that reflects Christ to the world. Remember, you may be the only Christlike example that your child sees. Let your light shine so that others see Christ in you.

Now therefore, please be careful not to drink wine or similar drink, and not to eat anything unclean. For behold, you shall conceive and bear a son. And no razor shall come upon his head, for the child shall be a Nazirite to God from the womb; and he shall begin to deliver Israel out of the hand of the Philistines.

—JUDGES 13:4–5

But as for you, speak the things which are proper for sound doctrine . . . the older women likewise, that they be reverent in behavior, not slanderers, not given to much wine, teachers of good things—that they admonish the young women to love their husbands, to love their children, to be discreet, chaste, homemakers, good, obedient to their own husbands, that the word of God may not be blasphemed . . . in all things showing yourself to be a pattern of good works; in doctrine showing integrity, reverence, incorruptibility.

—TITUS 2:1, 3–5, 7

Faith

Faith is our belief and trust in God. It is also our loyalty to God. When we have faith in God, we rely on Him and not on ourselves or on the world. Your faith is an important part of who you are in life and in the Lord. When you demonstrate your faith through the way you interact daily with others and by putting your complete trust in God, the love of Christ will shine through. When you walk by faith and not by sight, when you don't know what the future holds but you trust that God has your life in His hands, you walk with the Lord's light, which shines through in your actions. Your children are watching, and if you want to influence them for the glory of God, let your faith be evident in all that you say and do.

Then she came and worshiped Him, saying, "Lord, help me!" . . . Then Jesus answered and said to her, "O woman, great is your faith! Let it be to you as you desire." And her daughter was healed from that very hour.

—MATTHEW 15:25, 28

Now faith is the substance of things hoped for, the evidence of things not seen. For by it the elders obtained a good testimony.

—HEBREWS 11:1–2

The LORD repay your work, and a full reward be given you by the LORD God of Israel, under whose wings you have come for refuge.

—RUTH 2:12

And He said to her, "Daughter, your faith has made you well. Go in peace, and be healed of your affliction."

—MARK 5:34

Godliness

Godliness is our devotion to God. Being godly means behaving in ways that show our dedication to God. When you act in a manner that displays the character of God in your life, you demonstrate godliness. When others see Christ in you and see that you know Him, all that you say and do will demonstrate that God lives in your heart. You will be an example of someone who is devoted to the Lord. Having a support system will help you continue on the path God has chosen for you. Because of this, strive to have godly friends who will help you to develop a character of godliness. Spend time with people who encourage you to be mindful of your thoughts, words, and actions. The Lord has called you to be a witness to others so that people will see Christ in you. When you live life in such a way that Christ is first and foremost in your life, you will be blessed.

It is written, "Be holy, for I am holy."

—1 Peter 1:16

In like manner also, that the women adorn themselves in modest apparel, with propriety and moderation, not with braided hair or gold or pearls or costly clothing, but, which is proper for women professing godliness, with good works.

—1 Timothy 2:9–10

But reject profane and old wives' fables, and exercise yourself toward godliness. For bodily exercise profits a little, but godliness is profitable for all things, having promise of the life that now is and of that which is to come. This is a faithful saying and worthy of all acceptance. For to this end we both labor and suffer reproach, because we trust in the living God, who is the Savior of all men, especially of those who believe.

—1 Timothy 4:7–10

Home

For most of us, home is a special place, a place we long for when we are away. God longs to make His home in you, to abide in you. The Word of God says, "If anyone loves Me, he will keep My word; and My Father will love him, and We will come to him and make Our home with him" (John 14:23). As you seek to establish a loving, caring home, it is important that you develop a relationship with the Lord. The Lord wants very much to be involved with you. Invite Him into your heart and let Him be the master of your life. When you do, He will help to make your home a special place because He will live in your heart and help you create a loving home with and for your children.

She watches over the ways of her household,
And does not eat the bread of idleness.

—Proverbs 31:27

Honor widows who are really widows. But if any
widow has children or grandchildren, let them first
learn to show piety at home and to repay their parents;
for this is good and acceptable before God. Now she
who is really a widow, and left alone, trusts in God and
continues in supplications and prayers night and day.

—1 Timothy 5:3–5

The older women likewise, that they be reverent in
behavior, not slanderers, not given to much wine,
teachers of good things—that they admonish the
young women to love their husbands, to love their
children, to be discreet, chaste, homemakers, good,
obedient to their own husbands, that the word of God
may not be blasphemed.

—Titus 2:3–5

Love

The word *love* has many definitions and is used in many ways, but Christian love is based on the love God gives to His children. This meaning of the word *love* comes from the Greek word *agape*. *Agape* is not an emotion but a willful, acting love. *Agape* seeks to give with no thought of receiving. It is sacrificial love given in joy. This word *love* has great meaning for how you live your life. When you demonstrate God's love toward your children and to your entire family, you share a love that seeks no return. This is the love that Christ has for you as you allow His love to shine through you for your entire family. When you do this, the relationship you have with your children and family will be rich and full of His glory.

*Jesus answered him, "The first of all the commandments is: 'Hear, O Israel, the L*ORD *our God, the L*ORD *is one. And you shall love the L*ORD *your God with all your heart, with all your soul, with all your mind, and with all your strength.' This is the first commandment. And the second, like it, is this: 'You shall love your neighbor as yourself.' There is no other commandment greater than these."*

—MARK 12:29–31

Love has been perfected among us in this: that we may have boldness in the day of judgment; because as He is, so are we in this world. There is no fear in love; but perfect love casts out fear, because fear involves torment. But he who fears has not been made perfect in love. We love Him because He first loved us.

—1 JOHN 4:17–19

Watch, stand fast in the faith, be brave, be strong. Let all that you do be done with love.

—1 CORINTHIANS 16:13–14

Morality

Fashions come and go, but morals are unchanging. For Christians, being moral means exhibiting right behavior in the eyes of the Lord. The Lord calls you to be righteous and to live in such a way that you will honor your family and yourself. Practice living a life that is good and honest and show moral integrity in all that you do. Your family will be blessed. Proverbs 31:10 clearly says that a virtuous wife has far more value than rubies. When you live a pure life and you are married, you establish a trust with your husband and with God that cannot be broken. If you are tempted to breach your vows, veer from it and ask God to protect you. Pray that God will help you keep your eyes fixed on Him so that your morals will remain strong.

And they were both righteous before God, walking in all the commandments and ordinances of the Lord blameless.

—LUKE 1:6

The heart of her husband safely trusts her;
    So he will have no lack of gain.

—PROVERBS 31:11

Many daughters have done well,
    But you excel them all.

—PROVERBS 31:29

Then he said, "Blessed are you of the LORD, my daughter! For you have shown more kindness at the end than at the beginning, in that you did not go after young men, whether poor or rich. And now, my daughter, do not fear. I will do for you all that you request, for all the people of my town know that you are a virtuous woman."

—RUTH 3:10–11

Obedience

There is an old Christian hymn that says, "Trust and obey for there's no other way to be happy in Jesus but to trust and obey." In Deuteronomy 28, the Lord spoke to Israel and urged them to obey His voice. If they did so, He would set them high above all the nations of the earth. Today God urges you to obey His Word, and He promises to bless you when you do. God wants the best for you. He wants you to obey Him, pray to Him, and trust that He has the best plan for you. When you obey God and His laws, He will protect you, guide you, and go before you as you walk through life.

Oh come, let us sing to the Lord!

> *Let us shout joyfully to the Rock of our salvation.*
> *Let us come before His presence with*
>   *thanksgiving;*
> *Let us shout joyfully to Him with psalms.*
> *For the Lord is the great God,*
> *And the great King above all gods.*

—Psalm 95:1–3

Though He was a Son, yet He learned obedience by the things which He suffered. And having been perfected, He became the author of eternal salvation to all who obey Him.

—Hebrews 5:8–9

If someone says, "I love God," and hates his brother, he is a liar; for he who does not love his brother whom he has seen, how can he love God whom he has not seen? And this commandment we have from Him: that he who loves God must love his brother also.

—1 John 4:20–21

Prayer

Sometimes you may see prayer as an obligation, something you need to do. However, prayer is a gift from God. Through prayer, God invites you into a sacred relationship with Him. Prayer is an open window to Him. He wants you to come to Him and share your faults, hopes, and dreams. When you enter into a prayerful conversation with God, He will listen, and His Spirit will give you the guidance you need to serve Him faithfully. Prayer is essential to spiritual growth. Make a habit of coming to Him in prayer often. He is waiting for you to include Him in all that concerns you. When you give your whole heart to God and stay in constant communication with Him through prayer, God will bless you.

And Hannah prayed and said:

"My heart rejoices in the LORD;
>   *My horn is exalted in the LORD.*
>   *I smile at my enemies,*
>   *Because I rejoice in Your salvation.*
>   *No one is holy like the LORD,*
>   *For there is none besides You,*
>   *Nor is there any rock like our God."*

>   —1 SAMUEL 2:1–2

Then Solomon stood before the altar of the LORD in the presence of all the assembly of Israel, and spread out his hands toward heaven; and he said: "LORD God of Israel, there is no God in heaven above or on earth below like You, who keep Your covenant and mercy with Your servants who walk before You with all their hearts. You have kept what You promised Your servant David my father; You have both spoken with Your mouth and fulfilled it with Your hand, as it is this day."

>   —1 KINGS 8:22–24

Sacrifice

The word *sacrifice* has the same Latin root as the word *sacred*—holy, set aside for God. Psalm 51:17 says, "The sacrifices of God are a broken spirit, a broken and a contrite heart—these, O God, You will not despise." As you go through life, you may be faced with certain sacrifices that must be made. When you face these challenges, you can come to Him for answers and seek His guidance for how to deal with those problems. The Lord desires to be involved in your life. When you must make a sacrifice, take your concerns and questions to the Lord. He is ever ready to help you face whatever life brings. You are a child of the King, and He, more than anyone, understands sacrifice and has compassion on you during difficult seasons.

But Hannah did not go up, for she said to her husband, "Not until the child is weaned; then I will take him, that he may appear before the LORD and remain there forever." So Elkanah her husband said to her, "Do what seems best to you; wait until you have weaned him. Only let the LORD establish His word." Then the woman stayed and nursed her son until she had weaned him. Now when she had weaned him, she took him up with her, with three bulls, one ephah of flour, and a skin of wine, and brought him to the house of the LORD in Shiloh. And the child was young. Then they slaughtered a bull, and brought the child to Eli. And she said, "O my lord! As your soul lives, my lord, I am the woman who stood by you here, praying to the LORD."

—1 SAMUEL 1:22–26

I beseech you therefore, brethren, by the mercies of God, that you present your bodies a living sacrifice, holy, acceptable to God, which is your reasonable service.

—ROMANS 12:1

Thankfulness

Being thankful should be a way of life for all Christians. The Bible encourages us to be thankful in 1 Thessalonians 5:18: "In everything give thanks; for this is the will of God in Christ Jesus for you." When you have an attitude of gratitude and give thanks for the blessings God has bestowed upon you, your actions and life are lifted up. Take time each day to name your blessings. When you do this, you can't help but see the world as a glass half full and not half empty. When you are quick to whisper, *Thank You, Lord,* and teach your children to do the same, joy enters your heart, and you can celebrate the love that only Christ can give.

And Hannah prayed and said:

"My heart rejoices in the LORD*;*
*   My horn is exalted in the* LORD*.*
*   I smile at my enemies,*
*   Because I rejoice in Your salvation."*

—1 SAMUEL 2:1

Then Bathsheba bowed with her face to the earth, and paid homage to the king, and said, "Let my lord King David live forever!"

—1 KINGS 1:31

So she went in, fell at his feet, and bowed to the ground; then she picked up her son and went out.

—2 KINGS 4:37

Then Naomi said to her daughter-in-law, "Blessed be he of the LORD*, who has not forsaken His kindness to the living and the dead!" And Naomi said to her, "This man is a relation of ours, one of our close relatives."*

—RUTH 2:20

The Promises
of Motherhood

Abundance

A life abounding in the blessings of the Lord is a joyful life. The Lord wants the best for you. When you give yourself (your whole heart and soul) to the Lord, He will bless you abundantly. The Lord loves you with an everlasting love, and when you come to Him with an open heart, He promises to listen and hear your prayers. Take the time to come to the Lord in prayer and place your petitions before Him. A mother who knows the abundance of God's love is a blessing to her children. Therefore, let your soul delight itself in the abundance that God has promised to those who are faithful to His calling.

And they blessed Rebekah and said to her:

"Our sister, may you become
> *The mother of thousands of ten thousands;*
> *And may your descendants possess*
> *The gates of those who hate them."*
> > —Genesis 24:60

He shall come down like rain upon the grass before mowing,
> *Like showers that water the earth.*
> *In His days the righteous shall flourish,*
> *And abundance of peace,*
> *Until the moon is no more.*
> > —Psalm 72:6–7

And God is able to make all grace abound toward you, that you, always having all sufficiency in all things, may have an abundance for every good work.
> —2 Corinthians 9:8

Faithfulness

Faithfulness is steadfast loyalty to God, and it is the key to contentment when you walk hand in hand with the Lord. Hebrews 11:1 tells us that "faith is the substance of things hoped for, the evidence of things not seen." Take some time to read the honor roll of the faithful who are found in Hebrews 11. When faith, virtue, and knowledge are a part of your life, the Lord has promised to give you self-control, perseverance, and godliness. The Lord wants the best for those who are faithful and who live in His presence, and He wants very much to shower His love on you. Live each day faithful and devoted to His will, and He will bless you beyond all measure.

And it happened, when Elizabeth heard the greeting of Mary, that the babe leaped in her womb; and Elizabeth was filled with the Holy Spirit. Then she spoke out with a loud voice and said, "Blessed are you among women, and blessed is the fruit of your womb! But why is this granted to me, that the mother of my Lord should come to me? For indeed, as soon as the voice of your greeting sounded in my ears, the babe leaped in my womb for joy. Blessed is she who believed, for there will be a fulfillment of those things which were told her from the Lord."

—LUKE 1:41–45

For this reason we also, since the day we heard it, do not cease to pray for you, and to ask that you may be filled with the knowledge of His will in all wisdom and spiritual understanding; that you may walk worthy of the Lord, fully pleasing Him, being fruitful in every good work and increasing in the knowledge of God.

—COLOSSIANS 1:9–10

Grace

Grace is one of God's greatest gifts to mothers. It is entirely unmerited, for we have done nothing to deserve God's love, forgiveness, and salvation. The Lord has promised you grace when you walk hand in hand with Him. He has also promised that He will not withhold any good thing from those who walk uprightly with Him. God's grace is a gift given to those who have been saved through faith in Jesus Christ, and it is a gift freely given without exception. You need only to accept God's gift, confess that you are lost, and turn your life over to Him. Let your life be a reflection of His marvelous grace to your children, and live every moment for Him.

For by grace you have been saved through faith, and that not of yourselves; it is the gift of God, not of works, lest anyone should boast.

—Ephesians 2:8–9

For the Lord God is a sun and shield;
The Lord will give grace and glory;
No good thing will He withhold
From those who walk uprightly.

—Psalm 84:11

And the Word became flesh and dwelt among us, and we beheld His glory, the glory as of the only begotten of the Father, full of grace and truth. . . . And of His fullness we have all received, and grace for grace. For the law was given through Moses, but grace and truth came through Jesus Christ.

—John 1:14, 16–17

Guidance

God offers you His unlimited and unerring guidance when you trust in Him. As a mother, you are given the responsibility to guide your children so that they will grow and have lives that reach their full potential. God has placed within your heart the instinct and desire to lead your children to be fruitful in whatever they choose to do in life. Lean on the Lord. He has promised to give you the Spirit of truth to guide you. Trust the Lord to lead you in this endeavor of motherhood, and openly ask for His help each day. He will give you everything that you need to guide your children if you trust in Him with all of your heart.

Your ears shall hear a word behind you, saying,

"This is the way, walk in it,"
> *Whenever you turn to the right hand*
> *Or whenever you turn to the left.*

—Isaiah 30:21

"However, when He, the Spirit of truth, has come, He will guide you into all truth; for He will not speak on His own authority, but whatever He hears He will speak; and He will tell you things to come. He will glorify Me, for He will take of what is Mine and declare it to you."

—John 16:13–14

"The Lord will guide you continually,
> *And satisfy your soul in drought,*
> *And strengthen your bones;*
> *You shall be like a watered garden,*
> *And like a spring of water, whose waters do*
>> *not fail."*

—Isaiah 58:11

Honor

The key to social stability is buried in reverence and respect. When you live a life pleasing to the Lord, you build the respect due you as a mother. This means spending time in God's Word. It also means being patient and compassionate and disciplining your children wisely. When honor is a part of your character and of your daily life, your children will see that you are blessed, and they will want to follow your example. You will have a place of honor in your family, and they will listen to you when you speak and will give you the honor that you desire. Honor is given to you as you live out the life that God has planned for you. Being faithful to His calling and honoring God, brings bountiful blessings.

"Honor your father and your mother, that your days
may be long upon the land which the Lord your God
is giving you."

—Exodus 20:12

His glory is great in Your salvation;
    Honor and majesty You have placed upon him.
    For You have made him most blessed forever;
    You have made him exceedingly glad with
        Your presence.

—Psalm 21:5–6

Sing out the honor of His name;
    Make His praise glorious.
    Say to God,
    "How awesome are Your works!
    Through the greatness of Your power
    Your enemies shall submit themselves to You.
    All the earth shall worship You
    And sing praises to You;
    They shall sing praises to Your name."

—Psalm 66:2–4

Joy

Joy is a gift from God. It does not depend on your circumstances but on your relationship with God. When you walk with the Lord, He fills you with His presence, which enables you to have joy in every circumstance. Psalm 30:5 says that "weeping may endure for a night, but joy comes in the morning." Even during the hardships of motherhood, God longs to fill you with His joy. Stay close to Him and seek His guidance daily. Whether you are in a happy or trying season of motherhood, you can trust God to bless you with unshakeable joy. Determine to see the value and beauty in your present circumstances, and you will discover a new level of joy.

Though now you do not see Him, yet believing, you rejoice with joy inexpressible and full of glory.

—1 PETER 1:8

He grants the barren woman a home,
    Like a joyful mother of children.
    Praise the LORD!

—PSALM 113:9

Let your father and your mother be glad,
    And let her who bore you rejoice.

—PROVERBS 23:25

This is the day the LORD has made;
    We will rejoice and be glad in it.

—PSALM 118:24

Love

The Bible tells us that God loves all of His children, regardless of the choices we make. He showed this love to the Israelites, and He shows it to us today. God places within your heart a great love for your children. From the moment you became a mom, your world began to revolve around theirs. Your children are a part of you, and you nurture and care for them. You delight in them. Even when they have bad days, you love them. As your children grow, tell them often of your love for them. Share with them the unconditional love God has for them. Raising children who love God begins with the love that you plant in their hearts.

Though I have all faith, so that I could remove mountains, but have not love, I am nothing. . . . Love suffers long and is kind.

—1 CORINTHIANS 13:2, 4

And may the Lord make you increase and abound in love to one another and to all.

—1 THESSALONIANS 3:12

Beloved, if God so loved us, we also ought to love one another.

—1 JOHN 4:11

Let those also who love Your name
 Be joyful in You.
 For You, O LORD, will bless the righteous;
 With favor You will surround him as with a
 shield.

—PSALM 5:11–12

Prosperity

The world offers many good things, but the Lord wants what is best for you. He wants you to prosper in all that you do. To prosper means to thrive and flourish. When you faithfully serve Him and walk with Him, when you put your complete trust in the Lord, your life will blossom, and you will find success. Because the future is uncertain and focusing on it too much can bring about anxieties, allow the Lord to be your daily guide. Trust your future to Him. In your day-to-day life, the more you depend on Him and allow your thoughts to focus on Him, the more He will bless you. Trust in the Lord with all of your heart and not on your own power or understanding. When you acknowledge Him in all your ways, when you look to Him, He will direct your path and He will bless your life. This is a promise God has made to you.

For thus says the LORD God of Israel: "The bin of flour shall not be used up, nor shall the jar of oil run dry, until the day the LORD sends rain on the earth." So she went away and did according to the word of Elijah; and she and he and her household ate for many days. The bin of flour was not used up, nor did the jar of oil run dry, according to the word of the LORD which He spoke by Elijah.

—1 KINGS 17:14–16

Save now, I pray, O LORD;

    O LORD, I pray, send now prosperity.
    Blessed is he who comes in the name of the LORD!
    We have blessed you from the house of the LORD.
    God is the LORD,
    And He has given us light.

—PSALM 118:25–27

Provision

The Lord provides for His children. Because hardships are inevitable, you might experience worry or anxiety concerning how best to provide for your family. During these times, you can turn to God, and because of your trust and faith in Him, He will make a way for you to flourish. The Lord wants the best for you because He is a generous God, and He knows exactly what you need. Remember there is a difference between what you want and what you truly need. God will provide for you based on what He knows is right for you. You can trust that He will supply all that you need when you honor Him with your time and service. The blessings from the Lord are bountiful; therefore, walk with Him and place your life in His hands. He loves you with an everlasting love and will always provide for you when you follow Him.

Now there stood by the cross of Jesus His mother,
and His mother's sister, Mary the wife of Clopas,
and Mary Magdalene. When Jesus therefore saw His
mother, and the disciple whom He loved standing by,
He said to His mother, "Woman, behold your son!"
Then He said to the disciple, "Behold your mother!"
And from that hour that disciple took her to his
own home.

—JOHN 19:25–27

Then, being divinely warned in a dream that they
should not return to Herod, they departed for their
own country another way. Now when they had
departed, behold, an angel of the Lord appeared to
Joseph in a dream, saying, "Arise, take the young Child
and His mother, flee to Egypt, and stay there until I
bring you word; for Herod will seek the young Child to
destroy Him." When he arose, he took the young Child
and His mother by night and departed for Egypt, and
was there until the death of Herod.

—MATTHEW 2:12–15

Respect

It is important to God that children respect their mother. However, the respect that a mother receives depends on the type of life she leads. Respect is earned. The way you walk, talk, and treat others affects the respect shown to you. The words you say, what you don't say, how you act, and even your moments of inaction—whether positive or negative—also affect whether others do or do not respect you. Teaching your children respect is vital to a happy family, community, and society as a whole. Children who learn respect at home take care of their belongings, treat others with kindness and integrity, and listen to your guidance and leadership, just to name a few benefits of right teaching. When Christ shines in you through the way you treat others, then respect will come. You can be a model for your children, and in allowing Christ to live in your heart, you will show them that you are deserving of their respect.

"Every one of you shall revere his mother and his father, and keep My Sabbaths: I am the LORD your God."

—LEVITICUS 19:3

My son, hear the instruction of your father,
  And do not forsake the law of your mother;
  For they will be a graceful ornament on
      your head,
  And chains about your neck.

—PROVERBS 1:8–9

My son, keep your father's command,
  And do not forsake the law of your mother.
  Bind them continually upon your heart;
  Tie them around your neck.
  When you roam, they will lead you;
  When you sleep, they will keep you;
  And when you awake, they will speak with you.

—PROVERBS 6:20–22

Trust

The Bible encourages you to trust in the Lord with all of your heart. When you trust in the Lord, you believe that He is who He says He is. Your heart does not doubt in the Lord or in His power, love, and forgiveness. Psalm 37 expresses the importance of trusting God and doing good. When you are faithful to God, and you delight yourself in Him, He will give you the desires of your heart. You will likely experience situations when you feel afraid, but during these times, you can put your complete trust in God because He will never leave you. When you are weary and you don't feel as though you can handle one more thing, Jesus calls you to trust in Him and give Him your burdens. He offers you rest and comfort. You can teach this trust in God to your children as you live as an example of one who trusts God completely.

Trust in the LORD, and do good;
>   *Dwell in the land, and feed on His faithfulness.*
>   *Delight yourself also in the LORD,*
>   *And He shall give you the desires of your heart.*

>   —PSALM 37:3–4

Whenever I am afraid,
>   *I will trust in You.*
>   *In God (I will praise His word),*
>   *In God I have put my trust;*
>   *I will not fear.*
>   *What can flesh do to me?*

>   —PSALM 56:3–4

"Come to Me, all you who labor and are heavy laden, and I will give you rest. Take My yoke upon you and learn from Me, for I am gentle and lowly in heart, and you will find rest for your souls. For My yoke is easy and My burden is light."

>   —MATTHEW 11:28–30

Understanding

God never promises that we will understand Him, but we can ask Him for the wisdom and guidance to understand what He wants us to do in different life situations. When you walk with the Lord and depend on Him, the Holy Spirit will give you discernment. Discernment is a type of understanding that comes from the wisdom that only God can provide. Discernment is the ability to judge well based on your spiritual understanding. As a mother, your Christian life is important as you care for your family. You will encounter situations that you might be unsure how to handle. These are the times when you call on the Lord to give you wisdom and understanding, and He will provide. Do not hesitate to lean on Him during difficult times and when the road is unclear. When you include the Lord in your everyday life, He has promised to go before you and bless you. He will give you the understanding that you need to live for Him.

Discretion will preserve you;
  Understanding will keep you,
  To deliver you from the way of evil,
  From the man who speaks perverse things.

—PROVERBS 2:11–12

Through wisdom a house is built,
  And by understanding it is established;
  By knowledge the rooms are filled
  With all precious and pleasant riches.

—PROVERBS 24:3–4

And we know that the Son of God has come and has
given us an understanding, that we may know Him
who is true; and we are in Him who is true, in His Son
Jesus Christ. This is the true God and eternal life.

—1 JOHN 5:20

The Blessings
of Motherhood

Angels

Angels are God's messengers to us, and they watch over us. The Word of God speaks to us about the safety we will find when we abide in His presence. In Psalm 91:11, He has given us this promise: "For He shall give His angels charge over you, to keep you in all your ways." When you follow God, He offers His protection for your heart and your spirit. Spend time studying His Word and praying to Him so that you will have a strong, healthy relationship with Him. The Lord wants to protect you and keep you close. When you depend on Him, He will send His angels to guide you through life and to give you all the blessings you will ever need.

But the angel said to him, "Do not be afraid, Zacharias, for your prayer is heard; and your wife Elizabeth will bear you a son, and you shall call his name John."

—LUKE 1:13

Now in the sixth month the angel Gabriel was sent by God to a city of Galilee named Nazareth, to a virgin betrothed to a man whose name was Joseph, of the house of David. The virgin's name was Mary.

—LUKE 1:26–27

The Angel of the LORD said to her, "Return to your mistress, and submit yourself under her hand." Then the Angel of the LORD said to her, "I will multiply your descendants exceedingly, so that they shall not be counted for multitude. . . .

Behold, you are with child,
And you shall bear a son.
You shall call his name Ishmael,
Because the LORD has heard your affliction."

—GENESIS 16:9–11

Assurance

Through Jesus Christ, God gives you the assurance of salvation and life eternal. While you are on earth, the Lord is with you through every circumstance you find yourself facing. He will help you, defend you, strengthen you, and give you everything you need to live in His presence. Be assured that you can run to the Lord during times of trouble. Learn to depend on the Lord to give you wisdom and understanding. Remember the Lord wants the best for you. Listen to His Spirit as He guides you through life. You can be assured that if you follow Him, He will work out all the situations in your life, whether good or bad, to the glory of His name. You can rest assured that God is working all things togeter for our good.

*And we know that all things work together for good
to those who love God, to those who are the called
according to His purpose.*

—ROMANS 8:28

*Now faith is the substance of things hoped for, the
evidence of things not seen. . . . By faith we understand
that the worlds were framed by the word of God, so
that the things which are seen were not made of things
which are visible.*

—HEBREWS 11:1, 3

O God, my heart is steadfast;
    I will sing and give praise, even with my glory.
    Awake, lute and harp!
    I will awaken the dawn.
    I will praise You, O LORD, among the peoples,
    And I will sing praises to You among the nations.
    For Your mercy is great above the heavens,
    And Your truth reaches to the clouds.

—PSALM 108:1–4

Blessedness

The Lord wants very much to bless you with His love and to give you a joyful heart. As you open your heart to Him and seek His guidance, He will bless you and fill you with His love. You are a mother, and the Lord understands the love a mother has for her children. You are precious in the eyes of God, and He has blessed you with children. Listen and learn from Him, and let your life reflect His love for you. You are God's delight. Live in such a way that you will be a blessing to your family and to God. Then your children will understand how to live a faithful Christian life, and they will inherit blessings, for God said that He will show "mercy to thousands [of generations], to those who love Me and keep My commandments" (Exodus 20:6). God blesses those who obey Him and His Word.

"And I will bless her and also give you a son by her; then I will bless her, and she shall be a mother of nations; kings of peoples shall be from her." Then Abraham fell on his face and laughed, and said in his heart, "Shall a child be born to a man who is one hundred years old? And shall Sarah, who is ninety years old, bear a child?"

—GENESIS 17:16–17

And having come in, the angel said to her, "Rejoice, highly favored one, the Lord is with you; blessed are you among women!" But when she saw him, she was troubled at his saying, and considered what manner of greeting this was. Then the angel said to her, "Do not be afraid, Mary, for you have found favor with God."

—LUKE 1:28–30

And all these blessings shall come upon you and overtake you, because you obey the voice of the LORD your God.

—DEUTERONOMY 28:2

Children

The Bible says, "Children are a heritage from the LORD, the fruit of the womb is a reward" (Psalm 127:3). The presence of children in our lives is a blessing, and each individual child is a precious blessing from God. Give thanks to God every day for the wonderful gift of motherhood. One way you can bless your children is to teach them about God's love early in their lives, and let them know just how special they are to God. This is your responsibility, and when your children grow up knowing the love of Jesus Christ and when they accept Him as their personal Savior, you and your children will be blessed. Raising and guiding your children toward Christ is one of the most important tasks you can ever do.

Now Adam knew Eve his wife, and she conceived and bore Cain, and said, "I have acquired a man from the LORD." Then she bore again, this time his brother Abel. Now Abel was a keeper of sheep, but Cain was a tiller of the ground.

—GENESIS 4:1–2

How precious is Your lovingkindness, O God!
 Therefore the children of men put their trust
  under the shadow of Your wings.
 They are abundantly satisfied with the fullness of
  Your house,
 And You give them drink from the river of
  Your pleasures.
 For with You is the fountain of life;
 In Your light we see light.

—PSALM 36:7–9

Contentment

Being content in who you are and what you have been given in life is a gift that God gives to you. He has blessed you with the ability to accept right where you are in this moment and to find joy no matter the circumstance. God promises that He will "never leave you nor forsake you" (Hebrews 13:5). You can trust the Lord's promise. Therefore, let peace reign in your heart and learn to live each moment in His presence. This might seem like a challenging request if you are right in the middle of a difficult circumstance, but trust that God has already given you peace. All you have to do is believe Him and take His offered comfort. When you are content in the Lord, His love will shine through everything you say and do. The joy of the Lord will infect your children, and they will learn the peace that only God can give. Be content in who you are and what you are becoming. Be content and joyful in this very moment.

Now godliness with contentment is great gain. For we brought nothing into this world, and it is certain we can carry nothing out. And having food and clothing, with these we shall be content.

—1 Timothy 6:6–8

"Therefore do not worry, saying, 'What shall we eat?' or 'What shall we drink?' or 'What shall we wear?' For after all these things the Gentiles seek. For your heavenly Father knows that you need all these things. But seek first the kingdom of God and His righteousness, and all these things shall be added to you. Therefore do not worry about tomorrow, for tomorrow will worry about its own things. Sufficient for the day is its own trouble."

—Matthew 6:31–34

Family

God gives His children the gift of family. Mother, you are so blessed. God has granted you the gift of raising children in His family. You are a cocreator of your family, and you have the privilege of teaching your children how to live and how to act in the world. What you say and do for them will influence who they become. Shower your love upon them every day. Let them know often how much they mean to you. Let the words *I love you* be spoken daily. When you raise your children according to God's Word and you show them God's love, the love of Christ will shine through, and your children will be blessed. Your family will live fully in God's family.

He grants the barren woman a home,
    Like a joyful mother of children.
    Praise the Lord!

                     —Psalm 113:9

But Ruth said:

    "Entreat me not to leave you,
    Or to turn back from following after you;
    For wherever you go, I will go;
    And wherever you lodge, I will lodge;
    Your people shall be my people,
    And your God, my God."

                     —Ruth 1:16

"And when you go into a household, greet it. If the household is worthy, let your peace come upon it. But if it is not worthy, let your peace return to you."

                     —Matthew 10:12–13

Happiness

Psalm 146:5 declares, "Happy is he who has the God of Jacob for his help, whose hope is in the LORD his God." Two words in this verse demonstrate the meaning of happiness: *help* and *hope*. When you learn to come to the Lord and lean on Him for help in times of need, He promises to provide for you. When you trust in the Lord and place your hope in Him, He gives you peace. God's peace brings happiness and lifts your heart. A happy and lifted heart is contagious, and others are blessed by your joy. When you truly realize how blessed you are to be called a child of God, you will be filled with happiness. True joy is a gift that only God can give; therefore, look to Him, and He will give you happiness. Share this happiness with your family.

Then Leah said, "I am happy, for the daughters will call me blessed." So she called his name Asher.

—GENESIS 30:13

And you will have joy and gladness, and many will rejoice at his birth.

—LUKE 1:14

But let all those rejoice who put their trust in You;
　　Let them ever shout for joy, because You
　　　　defend them;
　　Let those also who love Your name
　　Be joyful in You.
　　For You, O LORD, will bless the righteous;
　　With favor You will surround him as with a shield.

—PSALM 5:11–12

Delight yourself also in the LORD,
　　And He shall give you the desires of your heart.

—PSALM 37:4

Healing

It is important to practice thankfulness when you are healthy in all aspects of your life. However, there will probably be times when you are sick and suffering. During these times, you can bring your concerns to the Lord because He is the Great Healer, and He will enable you to be thankful even in the midst of illness. In Jeremiah 33:6, the Lord spoke words of encouragement to the people of Judah when He said, "Behold, I will bring [the city] health and healing; I will heal them and reveal to them the abundance of peace and truth." The Lord offers healing to His children in many different forms because we don't all suffer in the same ways. God heals us physically, mentally, and spiritually, and He can make us whole again. Come to the Lord in prayer, and seek His comfort when you are ill or suffering and need healing. God is always available, and He will listen to your prayers.

Now when Jesus had come into Peter's house, He saw his wife's mother lying sick with a fever. So He touched her hand, and the fever left her. And she arose and served them.

*—*MATTHEW 8:14–15

And suddenly, a woman who had a flow of blood for twelve years came from behind and touched the hem of His garment. For she said to herself, "If only I may touch His garment, I shall be made well." But Jesus turned around, and when He saw her He said, "Be of good cheer, daughter; your faith has made you well." And the woman was made well from that hour.

*—*MATTHEW 9:20–22

But to you who fear My name
   The Sun of Righteousness shall arise
   With healing in His wings;
   And you shall go out
   And grow fat like stall-fed calves.

*—*MALACHI 4:2

Marriage

Marriage is a sacred gift from God, and it should be treated with reverence. When a man and a woman join together in holy matrimony, they are to become as one—caring about each other more than they care about themselves. When you do this, you allow your love for the other person to grow. This blesses your marriage as well as both of you. Marriage is the sacred foundation of the family. Think about the example God gives us for how to love each other. He loves you just as you are, with all of your faults and bad habits, as well as all of your wonderful traits. Christ sacrificed Himself for the good of the church He loved, giving us an example of how we are to love one another. You are called to sacrificially love your mate in the same manner.

Therefore a man shall leave his father and mother and be joined to his wife, and they shall become one flesh.

—GENESIS 2:24

It is good for a man not to touch a woman. Nevertheless, because of sexual immorality, let each man have his own wife, and let each woman have her own husband. Let the husband render to his wife the affection due her, and likewise also the wife to her husband. The wife does not have authority over her own body, but the husband does. And likewise the husband does not have authority over his own body, but the wife does.

—1 CORINTHIANS 7:1–4

Wives, submit to your own husbands, as to the Lord. For the husband is head of the wife, as also Christ is head of the church; and He is the Savior of the body. Therefore, just as the church is subject to Christ, so let the wives be to their own husbands in everything.

—EPHESIANS 5:22–24

Mercy

God's mercy stems from His compassion. He grants us His mercy even when we are undeserving. Numbers 14:18 says, "The LORD is longsuffering and abundant in mercy, forgiving iniquity and transgression." How wonderful that God continues to show His generous mercy no matter how we stumble and fall short of His desire for us. His mercy is new every morning, and you are blessed every day with His love. Therefore, praise the Lord and give thanks for His mercy, grace, and love. Be bold and share God's mercy and grace with others. By doing this, you will be more Christlike, and you will be an example of how to treat others. Remember, your children are watching how you conduct yourself in every situation you encounter, and they will learn compassion and mercy from you as you reflect God's love to the world.

*Then God remembered Rachel, and God listened
to her and opened her womb. And she conceived
and bore a son, and said, "God has taken away my
reproach."*

—Genesis 30:22–23

*And behold, a woman of Canaan came from that
region and cried out to Him, saying, "Have mercy on
me, O Lord, Son of David! My daughter is severely
demon-possessed." . . . Then Jesus answered and said
to her, "O woman, great is your faith! Let it be to you
as you desire." And her daughter was healed from that
very hour.*

—Matthew 15:22, 28

*But I have trusted in Your mercy;
    My heart shall rejoice in Your salvation.
    I will sing to the Lord,
    Because He has dealt bountifully with me.*

—Psalm 13:5–6

Power

Power can be used as a blessing or as a curse. Because you are a mother, your children are watching you, and often they mimic your behaviors, even when you don't realize it. Perhaps you have been blessed to be in a position where you have the ability to lead and direct others. If you use your power for selfish desires that hurt and affect others negatively, then that power becomes a curse. If you let the love of Christ shine through you, and if you are tender and thoughtful with what you say and how you act with others, then your power is a blessing to those around you. Your children see the way you treat others. Your actions impact and influence how they grow and develop their own personalities. If and when you are in a position to influence people and lead them, make sure you are using your power for the good of others and in a way that is pleasing to God.

She also rises while it is yet night,
*   And provides food for her household,*
*   And a portion for her maidservants.*
*   She considers a field and buys it;*
*   From her profits she plants a vineyard.*
*   She girds herself with strength,*
*   And strengthens her arms.*

—Proverbs 31:15–17

"But you shall receive power when the Holy Spirit has come upon you; and you shall be witnesses to Me in Jerusalem, and in all Judea and Samaria, and to the end of the earth."

—Acts 1:8

Yet in all these things we are more than conquerors through Him who loved us.

—Romans 8:37

Truth

*T*ruth is a powerful word. God's Word is truth, and it is the only source for holy truth. Being truthful isn't always easy because often we worry about hurting someone's feelings or offending others. Maybe you have felt uncomfortable living your life in a truthful way because it was different from how others were living around you. However, living a truthful life is essential to a healthy life, even when being truthful might be difficult. You can depend on the Lord to lead you in the way of truth. You can pray daily for the Lord to show you His ways and teach you His paths. The Bible has every answer you will need to live a life that reflects the love that Jesus has for you and your family. When you live a truthful life and you know the Truth, you will be free.

"If you abide in My word, you are My disciples indeed. And you shall know the truth, and the truth shall make you free. . . . Therefore if the Son makes you free, you shall be free indeed."

—JOHN 8:31–32, 36

"However, when He, the Spirit of truth, has come, He will guide you into all truth; for He will not speak on His own authority, but whatever He hears He will speak; and He will tell you things to come."

—JOHN 16:13

I have no greater joy than to hear that my children walk in truth.

—3 JOHN v. 4

Show me Your ways, O LORD;
      Teach me Your paths.
      Lead me in Your truth and teach me,
      For You are the God of my salvation;
      On You I wait all the day.

—PSALM 25:4–5

Scripture
Meditations
for Mothers

Meditations of Faith

Many are they who say of me,
"There is no help for him in God."
But You, O Lord, are a shield for me,
My glory and the One who lifts up my head.
I cried to the Lord with my voice,
And He heard me from His holy hill.
I lay down and slept;
I awoke, for the Lord sustained me.
I will not be afraid of ten thousands
of people
Who have set themselves against me
all around.
Arise, O Lord;
Save me, O my God!
For You have struck all my enemies on the
cheekbone;
You have broken the teeth of the ungodly.
Salvation belongs to the Lord.
Your blessing is upon Your people.
—Psalm 3:2–8

Be anxious for nothing, but in everything by prayer and supplication, with thanksgiving, let your requests be made known to God; and the peace of God, which surpasses all understanding, will guard your hearts and minds through Christ Jesus.

—Philippians 4:6–7

Therefore, having been justified by faith, we have peace with God through our Lord Jesus Christ, through whom also we have access by faith into this grace in which we stand, and rejoice in hope of the glory of God. And not only that, but we also glory in tribulations, knowing that tribulation produces perseverance; and perseverance, character; and character, hope. Now hope does not disappoint, because the love of God has been poured out in our hearts by the Holy Spirit who was given to us.

—Romans 5:1–5

Therefore we also, since we are surrounded by so great a cloud of witnesses, let us lay aside every weight, and the sin which so easily ensnares us, and let us run with endurance the race that is set before us, looking unto Jesus, the author and finisher of our faith, who for the joy that was set before Him endured the cross, despising the shame, and has sat down at the right hand of the throne of God.

—Hebrews 12:1–2

My soul, wait silently for God alone,
For my expectation is from Him.
He only is my rock and my salvation;
He is my defense;
I shall not be moved.
In God is my salvation and my glory;
The rock of my strength,
And my refuge, is in God.
Trust in Him at all times, you people;
Pour out your heart before Him;
God is a refuge for us.

—Psalm 62:5–8

God is our refuge and strength,

    A very present help in trouble.

    Therefore we will not fear,

    Even though the earth be removed,

    And though the mountains be carried into the
        midst of the sea;

    Though its waters roar and be troubled,

    Though the mountains shake with its swelling.

    There is a river whose streams shall make glad
        the city of God,

    The holy place of the tabernacle of the Most High.

        —PSALM 46:1–4

But you, beloved, building yourselves up on your most holy faith, praying in the Holy Spirit, keep yourselves in the love of God, looking for the mercy of our Lord Jesus Christ unto eternal life.

        —JUDE vv. 20–21

Meditations for Hope

Through the LORD's mercies we are not
consumed,
    Because His compassions fail not.
    They are new every morning;
    Great is Your faithfulness.
    "The LORD is my portion," says my soul,
    "Therefore I hope in Him!"
    The LORD is good to those who wait for Him,
    To the soul who seeks Him.
            —LAMENTATIONS 3:22–25

I would have lost heart, unless I had believed
    That I would see the goodness of the LORD
    In the land of the living.
    Wait on the LORD;
    Be of good courage,
    And He shall strengthen your heart;
    Wait, I say, on the LORD!
            —PSALM 27:13–14

"Hear, O Lord, and have mercy on me;
    Lord, be my helper!"
You have turned for me my mourning into
    dancing;
You have put off my sackcloth and clothed me
    with gladness.

—Psalm 30:10–11

We are hard-pressed on every side, yet not crushed;
we are perplexed, but not in despair; persecuted, but
not forsaken; struck down, but not destroyed—always
carrying about in the body the dying of the Lord Jesus,
that the life of Jesus also may be manifested in our
body. For we who live are always delivered to death for
Jesus' sake, that the life of Jesus also may be manifested
in our mortal flesh. So then death is working in us, but
life in you.

—2 Corinthians 4:8–12

Who shall separate us from the love of Christ? Shall tribulation, or distress, or persecution, or famine, or nakedness, or peril, or sword? As it is written:

> *"For Your sake we are killed all day long;*
> *We are accounted as sheep for the slaughter."*

Yet in all these things we are more than conquerors through Him who loved us. For I am persuaded that neither death nor life, nor angels nor principalities nor powers, nor things present nor things to come, nor height nor depth, nor any other created thing, shall be able to separate us from the love of God which is in Christ Jesus our Lord.

—ROMANS 8:35–39

"Come to Me, all you who labor and are heavy laden, and I will give you rest. Take My yoke upon you and learn from Me, for I am gentle and lowly in heart, and you will find rest for your souls. For My yoke is easy and My burden is light."

—MATTHEW 11:28–30

Therefore do not cast away your confidence, which has great reward. For you have need of endurance, so that after you have done the will of God, you may receive the promise:

> *"For yet a little while,*
> *And He who is coming will come and will*
> *   not tarry.*
> *Now the just shall live by faith;*
> *But if anyone draws back,*
> *My soul has no pleasure in him."*
>
> *—*HEBREWS 10:35–38

For our light affliction, which is but for a moment, is working for us a far more exceeding and eternal weight of glory, while we do not look at the things which are seen, but at the things which are not seen. For the things which are seen are temporary, but the things which are not seen are eternal.

> *—*2 CORINTHIANS 4:17–18

Meditations for Peace

"All your children shall be taught by the Lord,
And great shall be the peace of your
children.
In righteousness you shall be established;
You shall be far from oppression, for you
shall not fear;
And from terror, for it shall not come
near you.
Indeed they shall surely assemble, but not
because of Me.
Whoever assembles against you shall fall
for your sake."

—Isaiah 54:13–15

I will hear what God the Lord will speak,
For He will speak peace
To His people and to His saints.

—Psalm 85:8

"The LORD will guide you continually,
　　And satisfy your soul in drought,
　　And strengthen your bones;
　　You shall be like a watered garden,
　　And like a spring of water, whose waters do
　　　　not fail."

　　　　　　　　　　　　　　—ISAIAH 58:11

Let the words of my mouth and the meditation of my
heart
　　Be acceptable in Your sight,
　　O LORD, my strength and my Redeemer.

　　　　　　　　　　　　　　—PSALM 19:14

Be anxious for nothing, but in everything by prayer
and supplication, with thanksgiving, let your requests
be made known to God; and the peace of God, which
surpasses all understanding, will guard your hearts
and minds through Christ Jesus.

　　　　　　　　　　　　　—PHILIPPIANS 4:6–7

Meditations on the Power of God

"I am He who lives, and was dead, and behold, I am alive forevermore. Amen. And I have the keys of Hades and of Death."
—REVELATION 1:18

"But hold fast what you have till I come. And he who overcomes, and keeps My works until the end, to him I will give power over the nations—

> *'He shall rule them with a rod of iron; they shall be dashed to pieces like the potter's vessels'—*

as I also have received from My Father; and I will give him the morning star."
—REVELATION 2:25–28

Now I saw a new heaven and a new earth, for the first heaven and the first earth had passed away. Also there was no more sea. Then I, John, saw the holy city, New Jerusalem, coming down out of heaven from God, prepared as a bride adorned for her husband. And I heard a loud voice from heaven saying, "Behold, the tabernacle of God is with men, and He will dwell with them, and they shall be His people. God Himself will be with them and be their God. And God will wipe away every tear from their eyes; there shall be no more death, nor sorrow, nor crying. There shall be no more pain, for the former things have passed away." Then He who sat on the throne said, "Behold, I make all things new." And He said to me, "Write, for these words are true and faithful." And He said to me, "It is done! I am the Alpha and the Omega, the Beginning and the End. I will give of the fountain of the water of life freely to him who thirsts. He who overcomes shall inherit all things, and I will be his God and he shall be My son."

—Revelation 21:1–7

Meditations of Praise

My heart is steadfast, O God, my heart is
        steadfast;
   I will sing and give praise.
   Awake, my glory!
   Awake, lute and harp!
   I will awaken the dawn.
   I will praise You, O Lord, among the
        peoples;
   I will sing to You among the nations.
                —Psalm 57:7–9

Oh, give thanks to the Lord, for He is good!
   For His mercy endures forever.
   Oh, give thanks to the God of gods!
   For His mercy endures forever.
   Oh, give thanks to the Lord of lords!
   For His mercy endures forever: . . .
   Oh, give thanks to the God of heaven!
   For His mercy endures forever.
              —Psalm 136:1–3, 26

Let the saints be joyful in glory;
   Let them sing aloud on their beds.
   Let the high praises of God be in their mouth,
   And a two-edged sword in their hand.

—PSALM 149:5–6

*Praise the L*ORD*!*
   Praise God in His sanctuary;
   Praise Him in His mighty firmament!
   Praise Him for His mighty acts;
   Praise Him according to His excellent greatness!
   Praise Him with the sound of the trumpet;
   Praise Him with the lute and harp!
   Praise Him with the timbrel and dance;
   Praise Him with stringed instruments and flutes!
   Praise Him with loud cymbals;
   Praise Him with clashing cymbals!
   *Let everything that has breath praise the L*ORD*.*
   *Praise the L*ORD*!*

—PSALM 150

Meditations for Trust

Those who trust in the Lord
 Are like Mount Zion,
 Which cannot be moved, but abides forever.
 As the mountains surround Jerusalem,
 So the Lord surrounds His people
 From this time forth and forever.
 For the scepter of wickedness shall not rest
 On the land allotted to the righteous,
 Lest the righteous reach out their hands to
  iniquity.
 Do good, O Lord, to those who are good,
 And to those who are upright in their hearts.
    —Psalm 125:1–4

Trust in the Lord with all your heart,
 And lean not on your own understanding;
 In all your ways acknowledge Him,
 And He shall direct your paths.
    —Proverbs 3:5–6

Lord, how they have increased who trouble me!
    Many are they who rise up against me.
    Many are they who say of me,
    "There is no help for him in God."
    But You, O Lord, are a shield for me,
    My glory and the One who lifts up my head.
    I cried to the Lord with my voice,
    And He heard me from His holy hill.
    I lay down and slept;
    I awoke, for the Lord sustained me.
    I will not be afraid of ten thousands of people
    Who have set themselves against me all around.
    Arise, O Lord;
    Save me, O my God!
    For You have struck all my enemies on the
        cheekbone
    You have broken the teeth of the ungodly.
    Salvation belongs to the Lord.
    Your blessing is upon Your people.

                        —Psalm 3:1–8

Meditations for Victory

To You, O LORD, I lift up my soul.
O my God, I trust in You;
Let me not be ashamed;
Let not my enemies triumph over me.

—PSALM 25:1–2

The righteous cry out, and the LORD hears,
And delivers them out of all their troubles.
The LORD is near to those who have a
broken heart,
And saves such as have a contrite spirit.
Many are the afflictions of the righteous,
But the LORD delivers him out of them all.

—PSALM 34:17–19

"Have I not commanded you? Be strong and
of good courage; do not be afraid, nor be
dismayed, for the LORD your God is with you
wherever you go."

—JOSHUA 1:9

Blessed is he who considers the poor;

The Lord will deliver him in time of trouble.

The Lord will preserve him and keep him alive,

And he will be blessed on the earth;

You will not deliver him to the will of his enemies.

The Lord will strengthen him on his bed of
illness;

You will sustain him on his sickbed.

—Psalm 41:1–3

In this you greatly rejoice . . . that the genuineness
of your faith, being much more precious than gold
that perishes, though it is tested by fire, may be found
to praise, honor, and glory at the revelation of Jesus
Christ, whom having not seen you love. Though now
you do not see Him, yet believing, you rejoice with
joy inexpressible and full of glory, receiving the end of
your faith—the salvation of your souls.

—1 Peter 1:6–9

God's Answers
for Mothers

How to Be Christ-Centered

A Christ-centered life is one that is totally committed to Jesus Christ. Placing Him first in your life is a choice, and developing a relationship with God that cannot be broken is a choice. When you make these choices, God will touch your heart, and you will have the peace that your heart has always longed for. The time you spend in prayer and meditation will be rich, and this richness will, in turn, bless your life and all who are a part of it. When you live a life devoted to Christ, you will become a wonderful, loving mother filled with the Holy Spirit. Your children will learn how to live a Christ-centered life by watching you, and their lives will also be blessed.

And now, little children, abide in Him, that when He appears, we may have confidence and not be ashamed before Him at His coming.

—1 John 2:28

For the grace of God that brings salvation has appeared to all men, teaching us that, denying ungodliness and worldly lusts, we should live soberly, righteously, and godly in the present age, looking for the blessed hope and glorious appearing of our great God and Savior Jesus Christ.

—Titus 2:11–13

In You, O Lord, I put my trust;
 Let me never be put to shame. . . .
 For You are my hope, O Lord God;
 You are my trust from my youth. . . .
 Let my mouth be filled with Your praise
 And with Your glory all the day.

—Psalm 71:1, 5, 8

How to Build a Life of Prayer

When a mother opens her heart to God and spends time with Him in prayer, He has promised to listen and to answer her prayers. The relationship you have with God will depend on the depth of your prayer life and how committed you are to having a consistent and healthy prayer life. Remember that prayer is God's gift to you. Almighty God wants a relationship with you, and prayer is the way you communicate with Him. Just as God listens to you, He wants you to listen to Him. Proverbs 1:33 says, "Whoever listens to me will dwell safely, and will be secure, without fear of evil." Therefore, develop a consistent prayer life that includes God in every area of your life, no matter how small, unimportant, or shameful you think it might be. He is waiting to hear from you.

As for me, I will call upon God,
  And the Lord shall save me.
  Evening and morning and at noon
  I will pray, and cry aloud,
  And He shall hear my voice.

—Psalm 55:16–17

Let us therefore come boldly to the throne of grace,
that we may obtain mercy and find grace to help in
time of need.

—Hebrews 4:16

You will make your prayer to Him,
  He will hear you,
  And you will pay your vows.
  You will also declare a thing,
  And it will be established for you;
  So light will shine on your ways.

—Job 22:27–28

How to Deal with Suffering

As a mother, you will face times of suffering due to life situations. Some of these situations might be dealing with the illnesses of your children or with disappointments you feel because of family members. God wants you to know that He will carry you through these seasons of your life. First Peter 2:21 says that Christ "suffered for us, leaving us an example, that you should follow His steps." As you suffer, remember that Jesus is your example in all things, even in suffering. He did not willingly suffer for suffering's sake, but He accepted it because He saw it as God's will for Him. God teaches you through life experiences to depend on Him for guidance and understanding. In doing this, you can become more like Jesus in every way. If you let them, your sufferings can draw you nearer to God.

For our light affliction, which is but for a moment,
is working for us a far more exceeding and eternal
weight of glory, while we do not look at the things
which are seen, but at the things which are not seen.
For the things which are seen are temporary, but the
things which are not seen are eternal.

—2 CORINTHIANS 4:17–18

But may the God of all grace, who called us to His
eternal glory by Christ Jesus, after you have suffered
a while, perfect, establish, strengthen, and settle you.
To Him be the glory and the dominion forever and
ever. Amen.

—1 PETER 5:10–11

[We are] heirs of God and joint heirs with Christ,
if indeed we suffer with Him, that we may also be
glorified together. For I consider that the sufferings of
this present time are not worthy to be compared with
the glory which shall be revealed in us.

—ROMANS 8:17–18

How to Face Trials

The Lord is your protector. When trials come through your door, you can run to Him. He is the One who cares for you—more than you know and more than you could ever imagine. First Peter 5:7 says to "[cast] all your care upon Him, for He cares for you." When you do cast all your concerns and worries on Him, the Lord will comfort you and give you His peace. This is a peace that only God can give, a peace that will sustain you no matter how difficult the hardship becomes. This is the kind of peace your heart has always longed for, and you cannot find it in people or in the world. It is the peace of God. The Lord has promised to be with you when you face trials and tribulations. If you trust in the Lord with all of your heart, He will never leave you nor forsake you, and that alone will offer you comfort as you face trials.

Yea, though I walk through the valley of the shadow
of death,
I will fear no evil;
For You are with me;
Your rod and Your staff, they comfort me.
—P<small>SALM</small> 23:4

And He said to me, "My grace is sufficient for you, for
My strength is made perfect in weakness." Therefore
most gladly I will rather boast in my infirmities, that
the power of Christ may rest upon me.
—2 C<small>ORINTHIANS</small> 12:9

The righteous cry out, and the L<small>ORD</small> *hears,*
And delivers them out of all their troubles.
The L<small>ORD</small> *is near to those who have a broken heart,*
And saves such as have a contrite spirit.
Many are the afflictions of the righteous,
But the L<small>ORD</small> *delivers him out of them all.*
—P<small>SALM</small> 34:17–19

How to Grasp the Power of the Word

The Bible declares that the words of the Lord are pure and living and powerful and sharper than any two-edged sword. When you spend time in thought and meditation, the Word of God will come alive in your spirit. You will feel God's Word in your heart, not just know it in your mind. Study God's Word, and follow David's example: "Your word have I hidden in my heart" (Psalm 119:11). When you learn more and more about God's Word, it becomes easier to grasp the power of His Word. You will gain discernment as to how to apply the Word in your life. As you read and meditate on the Word, remember that the Bible is your guide for life. On its pages are the answers you will need to live a life that is fruitful for the Lord, and the power of God's Word will come alive in your heart.

The words of the LORD are pure words,
    Like silver tried in a furnace of earth,
    Purified seven times.
    You shall keep them, O LORD,
    You shall preserve them from this generation
        forever.

    —PSALM 12:6–7

All Scripture is given by inspiration of God, and is
profitable for doctrine, for reproof, for correction, for
instruction in righteousness.

    —2 TIMOTHY 3:16

For the word of God is living and powerful, and
sharper than any two-edged sword, piercing even
to the division of soul and spirit, and of joints and
marrow, and is a discerner of the thoughts and intents
of the heart.

    —HEBREWS 4:12

How to Have the Joy of the Lord

Psalm 89:15–17 says, "Blessed are the people who know the joyful sound! They walk, O LORD, in the light of Your countenance. In Your name they rejoice all day long, and in Your righteousness they are exalted. For You are the glory of their strength, and in Your favor our horn is exalted." When you exalt the Lord and live according to His will, joy is one of the fruits of your labor. The Lord wants you to be happy and joyful, filled with praise for His holy name. When you are consciously thankful for the Lord's blessings, and you go throughout your day being grateful, joy will fill your heart, and your children will reap the benefits. The Lord wants to hear your praises, and He is pleased with your thanksgiving. When you are joyful, the love of God will shine through you in everything you say and do.

"Come to Me, all you who labor and are heavy laden, and I will give you rest. Take My yoke upon you and learn from Me, for I am gentle and lowly in heart, and you will find rest for your souls. For My yoke is easy and My burden is light."

—Matthew 11:28–30

Create in me a clean heart, O God,
    And renew a steadfast spirit within me.
    Do not cast me away from Your presence,
    And do not take Your Holy Spirit from me.
    Restore to me the joy of Your salvation,
    And uphold me by Your generous Spirit.

—Psalm 51:10–12

You will show me the path of life;
    In Your presence is fullness of joy;
    At Your right hand are pleasures forevermore.

—Psalm 16:11

How to Hold on to Your Faith

Holding on to your faith requires placing the Lord first in your life and learning to live in His presence. In life there will be many distractions and temptations that will try to pull you away from God, but remember that your job is to focus on the Lord in spite of those distractions. The best way to walk hand in hand with God is to accept the fact that you must give the Lord His rightful place in your life. The Lord must come before everyone and everything else in your life. You must make Him your first priority. Like a tree without its water source that is barren or withers away, you will not bear fruit without the Lord as the Source of your life. Make sure the Lord is at the center of your life. This will keep your faith strong and secure.

"Have I not commanded you? Be strong and of good courage; do not be afraid, nor be dismayed, for the Lord your God is with you wherever you go."

—Joshua 1:9

For with God nothing will be impossible.

—Luke 1:37

We are hard-pressed on every side, yet not crushed; we are perplexed, but not in despair; persecuted, but not forsaken; struck down, but not destroyed—always carrying about in the body the dying of the Lord Jesus, that the life of Jesus also may be manifested in our body.

—2 Corinthians 4:8–10

For we walk by faith, not by sight.

—2 Corinthians 5:7

How to Obtain God's Promises

The Bible is full of God's promises to you. God's promises are guiding lights for you to follow. God has already provided everything you need to become more like Christ. You do not need a new experience or a grand revelation to help you draw closer to God—although sometimes major life changes or heartbreaking experiences bring us closer to Him. Whether your life is going well at the moment or you are experiencing a tough time, you can use what He has already given. Take some time to study the Bible and discover the promises God has made to you. Jesus wants your spiritual life to grow and become fruitful because He knows that a righteous life greatly pleases the Father, gives you enormous satisfaction, and results in children who are far more likely to pursue Him as they mature.

[We have been given] exceedingly great and precious promises, that through these you may be partakers of the divine nature, having escaped the corruption that is in the world through lust. But also for this very reason, giving all diligence, add to your faith virtue, to virtue knowledge, to knowledge self-control, to self-control perseverance, to perseverance godliness, to godliness brotherly kindness, and to brotherly kindness love. For if these things are yours and abound, you will be neither barren nor unfruitful in the knowledge of our Lord Jesus Christ.

—2 Peter 1:4–8

Let us hold fast the confession of our hope without wavering, for He who promised is faithful.

—Hebrews 10:23

"But seek first the kingdom of God and His righteousness, and all these things shall be added to you."

—Matthew 6:33

How to Overcome Despair

Despair is the loss of hope. Christians never need to despair because our hope is in the Lord. In Psalm 27:14 the Lord encourages you to "wait on the LORD; be of good courage, and He shall strengthen your heart; wait, I say, on the LORD!". In life you may find yourself impatient—particularly when you are faced with a despairing situation. You want quick fixes and easy answers, but these wouldn't allow you to heal the way God needs you to. God needs you whole, and sometimes covering up a hurt does not heal it; it merely hides it until it rises up again later. The Lord encourages you to wait on Him and to trust in Him. He offers you healing and a way out of despair. When you rely on the Holy Spirit to protect and guide you through life's difficult times, God has promised that He is for you, and nothing is impossible for Him!

But You, O Lord, are a shield for me,
    My glory and the One who lifts up my head.
    I cried to the Lord with my voice,
    And He heard me from His holy hill.
    I lay down and slept;
    I awoke, for the Lord sustained me.
    I will not be afraid of ten thousands of people
    Who have set themselves against me all around.
                  —PSALM 3:3–6

And He said to me, "My grace is sufficient for you, for My strength is made perfect in weakness." Therefore most gladly I will rather boast in my infirmities, that the power of Christ may rest upon me.
                  —2 CORINTHIANS 12:9

What then shall we say to these things? If God is for us, who can be against us?
                  —ROMANS 8:31

How to Overcome Stress

God has promised to be with you in times of stress. He promises to strengthen you, and He gives you reassurance that you can depend on Him. In 2 Timothy 1:7, Paul said, "For God has not given us a spirit of fear, but of power and of love and of a sound mind." Most of our stress originates from fears and worries we have about the future. You might have questions like, *What is going to happen? Can I get this done? Will everything work out?* These are your fears creating stressful thoughts, but Paul tells us that we have not been given a spirit of fear. You are priceless beyond measure to God, so much that He sent His Son to save you. He also enables you to experience contentment and freedom from stress by taking His yoke rather than your own, and by allowing Him to heal your mind.

"Peace I leave with you, My peace I give to you; not as the world gives do I give to you. Let not your heart be troubled, neither let it be afraid."

—JOHN 14:27

"Fear not, for I am with you;
 Be not dismayed, for I am your God.
 I will strengthen you,
 Yes, I will help you,
 I will uphold you with My righteous right hand."

—ISAIAH 41:10

God is our refuge and strength,
 A very present help in trouble.
 Therefore we will not fear,
 Even though the earth be removed,
 And though the mountains be carried into the
  midst of the sea;
 Though its waters roar and be troubled,
 Though the mountains shake with its swelling.

—PSALM 46:1–3

God Comforts
Mothers
as They
Learn To . . .

Be Content with Themselves

Contentment is a state of happiness and satisfaction. For Christians, being content in all things means being satisfied with what God provides. You will grow content when you learn to see God as your sole provider and you know that He will provide all that you and your family truly need. Knowing this will help you become content in your relationship with Jesus Christ. Paul said, "Not that I speak in regard to need, for I have learned in whatever state I am, to be content. . . . I can do all things through Christ who strengthens me" (Philippians 4:11, 13). Although it might sound difficult or impossible to find contentment during times of trouble, knowing and believing you have a God who loves you more than you can imagine and who provides for all of your needs is enough to give you peace.

"For the mountains shall depart
    And the hills be removed,
    But My kindness shall not depart from you,
    Nor shall My covenant of peace be removed,"
    *Says the L*ORD*, who has mercy on you. . . .*
    *"All your children shall be taught by the L*ORD*,*
    And great shall be the peace of your children."
            —ISAIAH 54:10, 13

Not that I speak in regard to need, for I have learned
in whatever state I am, to be content: I know how to be
abased, and I know how to abound. Everywhere and
in all things I have learned both to be full and to be
hungry, both to abound and to suffer need.

            —PHILIPPIANS 4:11–12

Now godliness with contentment is great gain. For we
brought nothing into this world, and it is certain we
can carry nothing out. And having food and clothing,
with these we shall be content.

            —1 TIMOTHY 6:6–8

Call on God's Divine Protection

There is safety in abiding in the presence of God. To abide in the presence of God means to remain steadfast and loyal in your praise, devotion, and trust of Him. Psalm 91:1–2 says, "He who dwells in the secret place of the Most High shall abide under the shadow of the Almighty. I will say of the LORD, 'He is my refuge and my fortress; my God, in Him I will trust.'" When you walk closely with the Lord, He will always be your protector. When you learn to follow His will and obey His commands, you will be blessed. Your children will see a mother whom they want to be like, and they will see how God takes care of His children. Your family will learn how to call on God's divine protection too. The Lord will surround you and your children with His love, mercy, and grace.

I will both lie down in peace, and sleep;
    For You alone, O Lord, make me dwell in safety.

        —Psalm 4:8

The Lord is my light and my salvation;
    Whom shall I fear?
    The Lord is the strength of my life;
    Of whom shall I be afraid?
    When the wicked came against me
    To eat up my flesh,
    My enemies and foes,
    They stumbled and fell.
    Though an army may encamp against me,
    My heart shall not fear;
    Though war may rise against me,
    In this I will be confident.

        —Psalm 27:1–3

But whoever listens to me will dwell safely,
    And will be secure, without fear of evil.

        —Proverbs 1:33

Confront Serious Illness

God sometimes uses a serious illness to draw us closer to Him. When you or someone in your family faces an illness, you can go to the Lord in prayer. You can tell Him about your concerns or fears or hopes. The Lord is always available to listen, guide, comfort, and heal us in His own time and in His own way. Even if you don't see immediate results, such as physical healing, keep on praying. God answers our prayers according to His will and in ways we cannot understand. The longer you pray for a loved one, the more tightly your heart will be bound to him or her. Prayer binds us together with a spiritual glue that is stronger than anything people can create. Such a bond lasts into eternity.

Heal me, O LORD, and I shall be healed;
Save me, and I shall be saved,
For You are my praise.

—JEREMIAH 17:14

The prayer of faith will save the sick, and the Lord will
raise him up.

—JAMES 5:15

Blessed be the God and Father of our Lord Jesus Christ,
the Father of mercies and God of all comfort, who
comforts us in all our tribulation, that we may be
able to comfort those who are in any trouble, with the
comfort with which we ourselves are comforted by God.

—2 CORINTHIANS 1:3–4

For this is God,
Our God forever and ever;
He will be our guide
Even to death.

—PSALM 48:14

Deal with Financial Stress

Sometimes financial difficulties arise in life, and this kind of stress is very taxing on the mind and body. There are times when problems are out of your control (such as a car accident or malfunctioning appliance), and other times financial difficulties are created when you aren't responsible with your money. If you do not relinquish control to the Lord, either situation can create anxiety and fear for you and your family. The Bible suggests that you examine what you do with the money you have. Are you responsible or are you reckless in your stewardship of money? When you are responsible with your finances and look to God for guidance, He will bless you. Jesus said, "I have come that they may have life, and that they may have it more abundantly" (John 10:10). Walk closely with the Lord.

Then He said to His disciples, "Therefore I say to you, do not worry about your life, what you will eat; nor about the body, what you will put on. Life is more than food, and the body is more than clothing. Consider the ravens, for they neither sow nor reap, which have neither storehouse nor barn; and God feeds them. Of how much more value are you than the birds?"

—LUKE 12:22–24

And the Lord said, "Who then is that faithful and wise steward, whom his master will make ruler over his household, to give them their portion of food in due season? Blessed is that servant whom his master will find so doing when he comes. Truly, I say to you that he will make him ruler over all that he has."

—LUKE 12:42–44

And my God shall supply all your need according to His riches in glory by Christ Jesus.

—PHILIPPIANS 4:19

Face the Year Ahead

Life is a teacher, and as a godly mother, it's likely you have learned to take your responsibilities seriously. The year ahead will hold many happy times and some times that are not as good. When life situations are difficult, you can turn to the Lord for wisdom and strength. He will guide you with love and instruction for your children. When you live in right standing with the Lord, His Spirit will direct your steps. You can rejoice in knowing that you walk with God, for He has promised to be your guide through life. Learn to lean on Him and to rest in His promises. The Lord wants the very best for you as you face the year ahead; make the Lord a priority and watch how He guides your steps.

The days of our lives are seventy years;
> *And if by reason of strength they are eighty years,*
> *Yet their boast is only labor and sorrow;*
> *For it is soon cut off, and we fly away. . . .*
> *So teach us to number our days,*
> *That we may gain a heart of wisdom. . . .*
> *Oh, satisfy us early with Your mercy,*
> *That we may rejoice and be glad all our days!*
> > —PSALM 90:10, 12, 14

For I know that my Redeemer lives,
> *And He shall stand at last on the earth;*
> *And after my skin is destroyed, this I know,*
> *That in my flesh I shall see God.*
> > —JOB 19:25–26

For none of us lives to himself, and no one dies to himself. For if we live, we live to the Lord; and if we die, we die to the Lord. Therefore, whether we live or die, we are the Lord's.
> —ROMANS 14:7–8

Handle Spiritual Trials

James 1:2–3 says, "My brethren, count it all joy when you fall into various trials, knowing that the testing of your faith produces patience." You know there is nothing joyful about trials, in and of themselves. There is no value in suffering for its own sake, but God uses both spiritual trials and suffering to test your faith so that you may learn to endure patiently. The next time you face a spiritual trial, instead of asking God for a way out, ask Him what He wants you to learn from that trial. Praise God because He might be trying to teach you something to enrich your life and draw you closer to Him.

*Who shall separate us from the love of Christ? Shall
tribulation, or distress, or persecution, or famine,
or nakedness, or peril, or sword? . . . Yet in all these
things we are more than conquerors through Him
who loved us. For I am persuaded that neither death
nor life, nor angels nor principalities nor powers,
nor things present nor things to come, nor height nor
depth, nor any other created thing, shall be able to
separate us from the love of God which is in Christ
Jesus our Lord.*

—ROMANS 8:35, 37–39

*But, beloved, do not forget this one thing, that with the
Lord one day is as a thousand years, and a thousand
years as one day. The Lord is not slack concerning His
promise, as some count slackness, but is longsuffering
toward us, not willing that any should perish but that
all should come to repentance.*

—2 PETER 3:8–9

God Freely
Gives to
Mothers . . .

Comfort in Troubled Times

Life is filled with trials and tribulations—problems that you have to deal with. You can trust in the Lord when trials hit. You can always be sure that God will come to your aid because it is His nature. He is the Father of mercies and the God of all comfort. When you turn to the Lord for comfort and peace during hardships, He is there for you. This is a way He trains you to comfort others and to point others to Him during their times of need. Your children will want you to comfort them when they face trials, and you will be equipped to do this if you have been trusting the Lord during all of life's situations. Learn from your times of trouble so you can be the mother God has called you to be.

Blessed be the God and Father of our Lord Jesus Christ, the Father of mercies and God of all comfort, who comforts us in all our tribulation, that we may be able to comfort those who are in any trouble, with the comfort with which we ourselves are comforted by God.

—2 Corinthians 1:3–4

You who have done great things;
    O God, who is like You?
    You, who have shown me great and severe
        troubles,
    Shall revive me again,
    And bring me up again from the depths of
        the earth.
    You shall increase my greatness,
    And comfort me on every side.

—Psalm 71:19–21

Courage to Be a Woman of Integrity

When you think of a legacy to leave your children, there is none greater than a personal record of godly integrity. Those who develop moral character bless their children with a gift that will last for generations. When you model integrity, you give your children an example they can follow. This will bless them in the years ahead. Sometimes it takes courage to live a life of integrity when others around you aren't. It's not always going to be easy to veer from the crowd, especially if they don't want the light of God shined on them. Being different can be challenging, but following God will always bless you. Find other godly women of integrity to support you. Let integrity guide you so that you can live a life pleasing to the Lord and so that your children can too.

The L<small>ORD</small> shall judge the peoples;
Judge me, O L<small>ORD</small>, according to my
righteousness,
And according to my integrity within me.
—P<small>SALM</small> 7:8

He who walks with integrity walks securely,
But he who perverts his ways will become
known. . . .
The mouth of the righteous is a well of life,
But violence covers the mouth of the wicked.
—P<small>ROVERBS</small> 10:9, 11

Keep my soul, and deliver me;
Let me not be ashamed, for I put my trust in You.
Let integrity and uprightness preserve me,
For I wait for You.

—P<small>SALM</small> 25:20–21

The Gift of Eternal Life

Eternal life is a wonderful gift God has given you. You can't pay for it or earn it. Eternal life is a free gift because He loves you with an everlasting love and wants the very best for you. Live each moment in His presence and bask in His love, knowing that you are saved and will spend eternity with Him. Your children will be blessed when they see the life of Jesus being lived out through you. Tell your children often about the love Jesus has for them, and help them understand the sacrifice that Jesus paid on the cross to save everyone. Thank God today for His gift of eternal life.

And we know that the Son of God has come and has given us an understanding, that we may know Him who is true; and we are in Him who is true, in His Son Jesus Christ. This is the true God and eternal life.

—1 John 5:20

But God, who is rich in mercy, because of His great love with which He loved us, even when we were dead in trespasses, made us alive together with Christ (by grace you have been saved), and raised us up together, and made us sit together in the heavenly places in Christ Jesus, that in the ages to come He might show the exceeding riches of His grace in His kindness toward us in Christ Jesus.

—Ephesians 2:4–7

For the wages of sin is death, but the gift of God is eternal life in Christ Jesus our Lord.

—Romans 6:23

The Peace That Only He Can Give

Paul told the Philippians, "Be anxious for nothing, but in everything by prayer and supplication, with thanksgiving, let your requests be made known to God; and the peace of God, which surpasses all understanding, will guard your hearts and minds through Christ Jesus" (4:6–7). Life is full of situations that tempt us to worry and doubt. You might often feel anxious about the circumstances you are in or that you think might be coming in the future. But worry and doubt will disappear when you take your cares to God because He has the power and wisdom to take care of them. Believe that He always has your best interests at heart. When you trust God with all of your needs, when you go to Him in prayer with a thankful heart, He offers you peace. God offers His peace to you every day; it's yours to reach out and grab.

For He Himself is our peace, who has made both one, and has broken down the middle wall of separation, having abolished in His flesh the enmity, that is, the law of commandments contained in ordinances, so as to create in Himself one new man from the two, thus making peace.

—Ephesians 2:14–15

You have put gladness in my heart,
> *More than in the season that their grain and*
>> *wine increased.*
> *I will both lie down in peace, and sleep;*
> *For You alone, O Lord, make me dwell in safety.*

—Psalm 4:7–8

The Lord will give strength to His people;
> *The Lord will bless His people with peace.*

—Psalm 29:11

Wisdom for Daily Living

The LORD gives wisdom; from His mouth come knowledge and understanding" (Proverbs 2:6). When you come to the Lord with an open heart and mind, seeking wisdom and understanding, He has promised that He will give you what you need to glorify Him. When you need guidance and direction for your children, come to Him in prayer, and He will supply your every need. Learn to listen to the Lord and allow Him to lead you. The Bible says in James 1:5, "If any of you lacks wisdom, let him ask of God, who gives to all liberally and without reproach, and it will be given to him." Trust that God will guide you every day and bless you with the wisdom to know how to teach and care for your family.

But the wisdom that is from above is first pure, then peaceable, gentle, willing to yield, full of mercy and good fruits, without partiality and without hypocrisy.

—JAMES 3:17

The fear of the LORD is the beginning of wisdom;
A good understanding have all those who do His commandments.
His praise endures forever.

—PSALM 111:10

How much better to get wisdom than gold!
And to get understanding is to be chosen rather than silver.

—PROVERBS 16:16

God Rejoices
with Mothers
When They . . .

Hope for Revival

Psalm 85:6–7 says, "Will You not revive us again, that Your people may rejoice in You? Show us Your mercy, LORD, and grant us Your salvation." In this sense, the word *revival* means an improvement in the condition or strength of your spirit. This kind of renewal is essential in any believer's life. Walk closely with the Lord and look to His Word for how to live. If you go your own way, using your own understanding, you will miss the blessings that He wants to bestow upon you. God desires to be involved in your life, and leaning on His understanding will lead you much further in life than you can go on your own. As a mother, when you continue to improve your faith and strength of spirit, you will be able to teach your children what it is like to walk hand in hand with the Lord. His gentle mercy will cover you with grace and love as you reach out to others in His name.

Arise, shine;
>   For your light has come!
>   And the glory of the LORD is risen upon you.
>   For behold, the darkness shall cover the earth,
>   And deep darkness the people;
>   But the LORD will arise over you,
>   And His glory will be seen upon you.

—Isaiah 60:1–2

All the ends of the world
>   Shall remember and turn to the LORD,
>   And all the families of the nations
>   Shall worship before You.
>   For the kingdom is the LORD's,
>   And He rules over the nations.

—Psalm 22:27–28

"And this gospel of the kingdom will be preached in all the world as a witness to all the nations, and then the end will come."

—Matthew 24:14

Join with Other Believers

You will experience comfort and joy when you fellowship with other believers. God desires for Christians to work in community with other believers and to serve others with our different ministries. We gain strength and reassurance from one another. When you join in fellowship with other believers, your faith will be strengthened, and you will have a sense of belonging. Each Christian has been given specific gifts that contribute to the health and well-being of the body of Christ. God created you to be unique, and you have specific gifts and talents. Therefore, find your place among those who believe in Jesus, and use your talents and gifts for the glory of God.

*God is faithful, by whom you were called into the
fellowship of His Son, Jesus Christ our Lord. Now I
plead with you, brethren, by the name of our Lord
Jesus Christ, that you all speak the same thing, and
that there be no divisions among you, but that you be
perfectly joined together in the same mind and in the
same judgment.*

—1 CORINTHIANS 1:9–10

*But God, who is rich in mercy, because of His great love
with which He loved us, even when we were dead in
trespasses, made us alive together with Christ (by grace
you have been saved), and raised us up together, and
made us sit together in the heavenly places in Christ Jesus.*

—EPHESIANS 2:4–6

*But you are a chosen generation, a royal priesthood,
a holy nation, His own special people, that you may
proclaim the praises of Him who called you out of
darkness into His marvelous light.*

—1 PETER 2:9

Live with Eternity in Mind

In Psalm 90:12 the psalmist wrote, "Teach us to number our days, that we may gain a heart of wisdom." Our minds are not made to completely grasp the concept of eternity, but there are ways we can live our days on earth with our hearts focused on God. As you live each day, look with anticipation for the Lord's return, and let every moment draw you closer to Him. Spend time studying His Word, and trust each day to God's capable hands. There will come a time when you will face your Maker, and you will want to hear, "Well done, good and faithful servant" (Matthew 25:21). How can you be a good and faithful servant? The Lord has said, "You will seek Me and find Me, when you search for Me with all your heart" (Jeremiah 29:13). Seek the Lord every day, and you will find Him. He will guide your steps and teach you how to be faithful.

He has made everything beautiful in its time. Also He has put eternity in their hearts.

—ECCLESIASTES 3:11

But know this, that in the last days perilous times will come: For men will be lovers of themselves, lovers of money, boasters, proud, blasphemers, disobedient to parents, unthankful, unholy, unloving, unforgiving, slanderers, without self-control, brutal, despisers of good, traitors, headstrong, haughty, lovers of pleasure rather than lovers of God, having a form of godliness but denying its power. And from such people turn away!

—2 TIMOTHY 3:1–5

For since the beginning of the world
 Men have not heard nor perceived by the ear,
 Nor has the eye seen any God besides You,
 Who acts for the one who waits for Him.

—ISAIAH 64:4

Seek His Sovereignty

God is sovereign over all things, which means that He has the ultimate power. Even though God is the supreme power over everything, He chooses to involve Himself in all areas of your life. God has chosen you to be in His family and to do His work in this world. As you use your talents, abilities, and training, God is with you, so seek His wisdom and guidance. You serve the God who is alive, who is present, and who gives life and breath to everything that lives. He is the ruler of the universe, and without Him, nothing exists. Therefore, seek Him and lift Him up with your praises. He is the God who was and is and forever will be your Lord and Savior.

Then Moses said to God, "Indeed, when I come to the children of Israel and say to them, 'The God of your fathers has sent me to you,' and they say to me, 'What is His name?' what shall I say to them?" And God said to Moses, "I AM WHO I AM." And He said, "Thus you shall say to the children of Israel, 'I AM has sent me to you.'"

—EXODUS 3:13–14

Great is the LORD, and greatly to be praised;
 And His greatness is unsearchable.
 One generation shall praise Your works to another,
 And shall declare Your mighty acts. . . .
 Your kingdom is an everlasting kingdom,
 And Your dominion endures throughout all
  generations.

—PSALM 145:3–4, 13

"Behold, I am the LORD, the God of all flesh. Is there anything too hard for Me?"

—JEREMIAH 32:27

Stand in Awe of the Lord

The meaning of the word *awe*, when referring to "standing in awe of the Lord," is a feeling of reverential respect mixed with fear or wonder. Having a fear of the Lord means you respect Him with a wholesome reverence rather than a feeling of terror or dread. When you have a healthy fear of the Lord, you honor and glorify Him to the extent He deserves. The Lord takes pleasure in those who revere Him. Choose to develop a respect for the Lord and understand that He is the giver and taker of all things. To please the Lord, you will want to live in such a way that God will be glorified in all you say and do. You have been bought with a price—the life of Jesus was given so that you could have fellowship with your Lord and Savior. As you stand in awe of the Lord, give thanks and praise His holy name.

If you seek her as silver,
  And search for her as for hidden treasures;
  Then you will understand the fear of the Lᴏʀᴅ,
  And find the knowledge of God.
                    —Pʀᴏᴠᴇʀʙs 2:4–5

He does not delight in the strength of the horse;
  He takes no pleasure in the legs of a man.
  The Lᴏʀᴅ takes pleasure in those who fear Him,
  In those who hope in His mercy.
                    —Psᴀʟᴍ 147:10–11

In the fear of the Lᴏʀᴅ there is strong confidence,
  And His children will have a place of refuge.
  The fear of the Lᴏʀᴅ is a fountain of life,
  To turn one away from the snares of death.
                    —Pʀᴏᴠᴇʀʙs 14:26–27

The fear of the Lᴏʀᴅ leads to life,
  And he who has it will abide in satisfaction;
  He will not be visited with evil.
                    —Pʀᴏᴠᴇʀʙs 19:23

God
Walks with
Mothers . . .

Through Adversity

Adversity is a part of life. We all must face it at some point in our lives. As a mother, you may face adversity yourself, or you may face it through your children. How you respond to adversity is what is most important. Your children will follow your example, and they will learn your habits and teachings. When faced with adversity, turn to God. He equips you to handle any situation that causes you pain or discomfort. As you release your problems to God, leave them there. Don't continue to drag them around and shoulder the burdens by yourself. Psalm 31 says, "In You, O LORD, I put my trust; let me never be ashamed; deliver me in Your righteousness. . . . For You are my rock and my fortress; therefore, for Your name's sake, lead me and guide me" (vv. 1, 3). When you lean on the Lord, He will walk with you through all of your troubles.

Beloved, do not think it strange concerning the fiery trial which is to try you, as though some strange thing happened to you; but rejoice to the extent that you partake of Christ's sufferings, that when His glory is revealed, you may also be glad with exceeding joy.

—1 Peter 4:12–13

Now thanks be to God who always leads us in triumph in Christ, and through us diffuses the fragrance of His knowledge in every place.

—2 Corinthians 2:14

And He said to me, "My grace is sufficient for you, for My strength is made perfect in weakness." Therefore most gladly I will rather boast in my infirmities, that the power of Christ may rest upon me.

—2 Corinthians 12:9

Through God we will do valiantly,
For it is He who shall tread down our enemies.

—Psalm 60:12

Through Disappointment

Have you felt disappointed? Most of us have been disappointed, whether in our families, in our children, or even in ourselves. Many times you want to handle your disappointments by yourself and not include God in the decisions you make. When you leave God out, you miss the opportunity to let His wisdom be your guide. When you talk to God about your disappointments, this is a big step in surrendering your life to Christ by allowing Him to be included in every part of your life. Give Him access to all of you and truly accept Him as your Lord and Master. Although people will continue to disappoint you—because no one is perfect—when you trust in the Lord, He will never disappoint. Romans 5:5 says, "Now hope does not disappoint, because the love of God has been poured out in our hearts by the Holy Spirit who was given to us."

Lord, I cry out to You;
>   Make haste to me!
>   Give ear to my voice when I cry out to You.
>   Let my prayer be set before You as incense,
>   The lifting up of my hands as the evening
>   sacrifice.

—Psalm 141:1–2

I have fought the good fight, I have finished the race, I have kept the faith. Finally, there is laid up for me the crown of righteousness, which the Lord, the righteous Judge, will give to me on that Day, and not to me only but also to all who have loved His appearing.

—2 Timothy 4:7–8

I know that whatever God does,
>   It shall be forever.
>   Nothing can be added to it,
>   And nothing taken from it.
>   God does it, that men should fear before Him.

—Ecclesiastes 3:14

Through Heartache

Psalm 147:3 tells us that God "heals the brokenhearted and binds up their wounds." When your heart is broken and you feel crushed by life's circumstances, you can talk to the Lord and share your heartache with Him. He has promised to listen to you and give you the rest and peace you desperately desire. Don't feel ashamed or too broken to go to the Lord. He loves you just the way you are, and He wants the best for you. God does not desire for your heart to be broken; He wants you whole and filled with love and joy. No matter how difficult your situation may be, you are precious in the eyes of the Lord, and He has the power to heal you. When you share your grief with God and come to Him with an open heart, He will give you peace. Do not hesitate to come to Him any time, day or night.

A man's heart plans his way,
*   But the Lord directs his steps. . . .*
*   The lot is cast into the lap,*
*   But its every decision is from the Lord.*

—Proverbs 16:9, 33

The Lord is near to those who have a broken heart,
*   And saves such as have a contrite spirit.*
*   Many are the afflictions of the righteous,*
*   But the Lord delivers him out of them all.*

—Psalm 34:18–19

"Come to Me, all you who labor and are heavy laden,
and I will give you rest. Take My yoke upon you and
learn from Me, for I am gentle and lowly in heart, and
you will find rest for your souls."

—Matthew 11:28–29

Through Impatience

It's not easy to see ourselves from God's perspective. He sees all that we have done in our lives. It can be a bit unsettling to think how many times we have disobeyed God. Yet God is patient and kind. He always forgives us when we confess and repent. If your children disappoint you and act in ways that frustrate you and make you angry, step back and be patient with them, just as God is patient with you. When your children try your patience, and you don't think you can take one more thing, remember how patient God is with you. Use the frustrating situation as a time to demonstrate your love as you correct your children. Proverbs 29:15 says, "The rod and rebuke give wisdom, but a child left to himself brings shame to his mother." Correct your children, but also be patient with them as they learn the difference between right and wrong. Let the Word of God be your guide.

My brethren, count it all joy when you fall into various trials, knowing that the testing of your faith produces patience. But let patience have its perfect work, that you may be perfect and complete, lacking nothing.

—James 1:2–4

Therefore be patient, brethren, until the coming of the Lord. See how the farmer waits for the precious fruit of the earth, waiting patiently for it until it receives the early and latter rain. You also be patient. Establish your hearts, for the coming of the Lord is at hand.

—James 5:7–8

Wait on the Lord;
Be of good courage,
And He shall strengthen your heart;
Wait, I say, on the Lord!

—Psalm 27:14

God Delights
in Mothers
Who Are . . .

Confident in Him

When you walk with God, you can be confident that He will be your guide and He will be glorified. Philippians 1:6 says, "Being confident of this very thing, that He who has begun a good work in you will complete it until the day of Jesus Christ." God is faithful to finish what He starts. Once you accept Christ as your Savior, the work of sanctification begins in you and is ongoing. There is always more to walking with God than what you have known, seen, learned, or experienced. As you study His Word, your confidence in Him will grow. Remain confident in the power and goodness of the Lord. Rest assured that He will always care for you because you are precious in His eyes.

*In You, O L*ORD*, I put my trust;*
Let me never be put to shame.
Deliver me in Your righteousness, and cause me
to escape;
Incline Your ear to me, and save me.

*—P*SALM *71:1–2*

*The L*ORD *shall preserve you from all evil;*
He shall preserve your soul.
*The L*ORD *shall preserve your going out and your*
coming in
From this time forth, and even forevermore.

*—P*SALM *121:7–8*

But Jesus looked at them and said to them, "With men
this is impossible, but with God all things are possible."

*—M*ATTHEW *19:26*

Forgiven by Him

When you come to the Lord with an open heart and seek forgiveness for your sins, He is faithful to forgive you and cleanse you from all unrighteousness. Psalm 103:12 says, "As far as the east is from the west, so far has He removed our transgressions from us." You are forgiven because of what Christ did on the cross, and you can stand boldly at the throne of grace and accept this love that Jesus Christ has for you. Let confession be a part of your daily prayer life. As you confess your sins, you open the window to heaven, and the Lord will hear your prayer and give you the guidance that you are seeking.

Now to Him who is able to keep you from stumbling,
And to present you faultless
Before the presence of His glory with exceeding joy,
To God our Savior,
Who alone is wise,
Be glory and majesty,
Dominion and power,
Both now and forever.
Amen.

—Jude vv. 24–28

If we confess our sins, He is faithful and just to forgive
us our sins and to cleanse us from all unrighteousness.

—1 John 1:9

Growing in Him

The Lord wants you to increase in wisdom and in your knowledge of Him. He always wants your relationship with Him to grow and strengthen. To do this, you will want to spend time in the Word and allow the Holy Spirit to fill your heart. You are called to be a witness for the Lord. This means that you are to share your love of the Lord with others, and you are to teach others about Him. This includes teaching your children about God and making sure they develop a strong relationship with Him. The more knowledge you have of the Word, the more you will grow in Him and the greater your impact on others will be. When the Bible speaks of letting your light shine so that others may see Christ in you, it is referring to how you express what your Christian faith means to you. Shine your light not only on friends and colleagues but also on your children and your family. Your family will grow and prosper in the Lord.

I will instruct you and teach you in the way you
     should go;
   I will guide you with My eye.

                    —Psalm 32:8

As newborn babes, desire the pure milk of the word,
that you may grow thereby, if indeed you have tasted
that the Lord is gracious.

                    —1 Peter 2:2–3

"This Book of the Law shall not depart from your
mouth, but you shall meditate in it day and night, that
you may observe to do according to all that is written
in it. For then you will make your way prosperous, and
then you will have good success."

                    —Joshua 1:8

"I am the vine, you are the branches. He who abides
in Me, and I in him, bears much fruit; for without Me
you can do nothing."

                    —John 15:5

Seeking Him

The Bible speaks plainly about seeking the Lord, and you are encouraged to seek Him every day. When a mother includes the Lord in her everyday life, she will be encouraged and comforted. God wants you to run to Him with your hopes, dreams, and desires. He wants to be included in your life. When your children see you reading your Bible and spending time with the Lord in prayer and meditation, they will want to do the same. The atmosphere you cultivate in the home will reflect the love of Christ. Proverbs 8:17 says, "I love those who love me, and those who seek me diligently will find me." Let your time with God be a priority in your life, and God will delight in you.

Seek the LORD and His strength;
Seek His face evermore!
Remember His marvelous works which He
has done,
His wonders, and the judgments of His mouth.
—1 CHRONICLES 16:11–12

I love those who love me,
And those who seek me diligently will find me.
—PROVERBS 8:17

I sought the LORD, and He heard me,
And delivered me from all my fears.
—PSALM 34:4

"But seek first the kingdom of God and His
righteousness, and all these things shall be added to
you. Therefore do not worry about tomorrow, for
tomorrow will worry about its own things. Sufficient
for the day is its own trouble."
—MATTHEW 6:33–34

Serving Him

The Bible mentions servanthood more than one hundred times. Jesus said that He did not come into the world to be served but to serve. We are called to do the same—to serve. John 12:26 says, "If anyone serves Me, let him follow Me; and where I am, there My servant will be also. If anyone serves Me, him My Father will honor." Serving Christ is an honor, and you must make an effort to serve God and others. If you want a closer relationship with the Lord, you will want to be involved with His church community so you can learn to serve the Lord faithfully while being supported by other believers. When you are involved in God's work, you will grow in your faith, and you will bless others. As you serve your family, do so with Jesus as your example, and your children will learn the value and importance of Jesus' mission of service.

And if it seems evil to you to serve the LORD, choose for yourselves this day whom you will serve, whether the gods which your fathers served that were on the other side of the River, or the gods of the Amorites, in whose land you dwell. But as for me and my house, we will serve the LORD.

—JOSHUA 24:15

And the people said to Joshua, "The LORD our God we will serve, and His voice we will obey!"

—JOSHUA 24:24

So the people asked him, saying, "What shall we do then?" He answered and said to them, "He who has two tunics, let him give to him who has none; and he who has food, let him do likewise."

—LUKE 3:10–11

Showing Him to Others

One of the privileges you have as a Christian is sharing your faith with others. When you allow your faith to come alive and you share your faith walk with those around you, you will bless them. Luke 11:33 says, "No one, when he has lit a lamp, puts it in a secret place or under a basket, but on a lampstand, that those who come in may see the light." You are God's light to the world. Let your light shine so that the world will see Jesus in you and want to learn more about Christ. Your light has the ability to change lives! Shine your light on your children and family too. You may be the only example of Christlike living that your children are exposed to. Let your light shine brightly. By living a life for God, your children will experience His love through you and they will understand that the Spirit lives in your heart.

Now by this we know that we know Him, if we keep His commandments. . . . But whoever keeps His word, truly the love of God is perfected in him. By this we know that we are in Him.

—1 John 2:3, 5

Therefore, having been justified by faith, we have peace with God through our Lord Jesus Christ, through whom also we have access by faith into this grace in which we stand, and rejoice in hope of the glory of God. And not only that, but we also glory in tribulations, knowing that tribulation produces perseverance; and perseverance, character; and character, hope.

—Romans 5:1–4

That which we have seen and heard we declare to you, that you also may have fellowship with us; and truly our fellowship is with the Father and with His Son Jesus Christ.

—1 John 1:3

Notes

....
....
....
....
....
....
....
....
....
....
....
....
....
....
....
....
....
....
....
....

Notes

Notes